Hands on PSHCE

Liz Webster
Sue Reed

Acknowledgements

The authors and publishers would like to thank the children of Aldingbourne Primary School for their enthusiasm, hard work and cooperation in the making of this book. Liz Webster, Headteacher of Aldingbourne Primary School and her Deputy Headteacher Sue Reed would like to thank all their staff for their cooperation and continued support. They would like especially to thank Wendy Davies for her hard work and commitment to helping put this book together. Sue Reed would like to express special thanks to her husband Ollie for his patience and for sacrificing his Sunday morning lie-ins. Finally, they would like to thank Steve Forrest, the photographer, for being absolutely gorgeous and always smiling during some very tricky photo shoots. A big thanks to everybody!

The Huge Bag of Worries (page 21)

Commissioning Editor: Zoë Nichols   Editor: Jill Adam
Page Layout: Barbara Linton   Photography: Steve Forrest
Cover Design: Steve West

First published in 2007 by Belair Publications.

Every effort has been made to trace the copyright holders of material used in this publication.
If any copyright holder has been overlooked, we should be pleased to make the necessary arrangements.

British Library Cataloguing in Publication Data. A catalogue record for this publication is available from the British Library.

ISBN 978 1 84191 4572

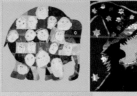

Contents

Introduction

Welcome to *Hands on PSHCE*. This book deals with the personal, social, health and citizenship education of primary aged children. Over recent years PSHCE has become a fundamental subject within every primary school's curriculum and ethos. The teaching of PSHCE develops the whole child and offers endless opportunities for discussion work that relates to children's real and future experiences.

This book aims to show how PSHCE can be taught and displayed in a creative, stimulating and fun way. By displaying PSHCE in your classroom and school environment, you are highlighting its importance. In this book we aim to demonstrate how to display PSHCE so that it is a valuable tool to enhance children's learning, to improve the quality of teaching for learning and to enrich the classroom environment.

Throughout this book we have demonstrated that the most effective PSHCE lessons are practical and exciting for the children. Each chapter offers a range of stimulating and original ideas that we use in our own classrooms – so we know they work! Each chapter relates to the PSHCE curriculum and focuses on issues that impact on every child's life. By addressing these issues at primary school age we are equipping the children with the tools necessary for dealing with future life experiences.

The emphasis within this book is not to produce written work but rather to engage children in lively discussions with their peers and to play fun and exciting games that will reinforce their learning and leave them wanting more.

Every theme in this book follows the same basic structure by including a whole-class starter, practical activities, art and display and cross-curricular links.

Whole-class Starter

This is the starting point for each theme and, to engage the children, must be exciting, stimulating and meaningful.

- In this book a wide range of the lessons have included the teacher 'in role'. This is an ideal way to capture children's interest and fire their imaginations. You may want to adopt the same 'persona' to carry on through several of the themes in the book. We have found that developing a character that the children come to know, particularly a character that is vulnerable, helps children to respond with honesty and a sense of compassionate responsibility.

- An effective teaching strategy that we have used repeatedly in this book is 'talk partners', with children in pairs discussing their ideas before sharing those ideas with the whole class. It acts as a support for less confident children as they may sound out their thoughts before expressing them to the larger group.

- Interactive games as part of the whole-class starter ensure that all learners and learning styles are catered for. Movement and action as part of a whole-class starter keep the children's attention and help to reinforce their learning.

- Visual props are a vital part of the whole-class starter, but they must be big, bold and colourful.

Practical Activities

- This part of the lesson reinforces the learning that has taken place during the whole-class starter session and it is vital that it is equally exciting.

- Children love playing games as they can get involved in them and become excited about their learning. Therefore, we have included ideas for table top games, carpet games and large area games.

- Where recording work is appropriate to reinforce key ideas or deepen children's understanding, it is essential that this recording is done in an imaginative way. Throughout the book we have mentioned a range of ways to record, for example, using shaped paper, zig-zag books, posters, spiral-bound books and so on.

Art and Display

Enjoying art in PSHCE lessons helps reinforce the children's learning in a creative way, using their imagination and practical skills. In this book we have identified art activities as part of every theme in order to consolidate their thinking and deepen their understanding. These art activities form the basis of many of the displays featured in the book. By displaying PSHCE within the school environment we are highlighting the importance of PSHCE as a fun and friendly subject to be enjoyed by children, and not one to fear.

Cross-curricular Links

We believe that making appropriate links to other subjects helps learning become more relevant and meaningful for young children. In this book we have highlighted ways in which these links might be possible in curriculum areas such as Science, Literacy, ICT, Maths, Design and Technology, Music and RE.

Above all, PSHCE should be:

Purposeful
Stimulating
Hands on
Creative and
Enjoyable for all!

PSHCE is fun and rewarding and if taught imaginatively it can make a real difference to every child because never forget... **EVERY CHILD MATTERS!**

Liz Webster and *Sue Reed*

The Healthy House

Whole-class Starter

- Jenny the schoolgirl (you in role) enters the classroom and tells the children that Nanny is looking after her and it is great because Nanny does not check up on what she is doing. Tell the class about your unhealthy (bad) habits, for example, not washing, going to bed with muddy knees, not eating your lunch, taking sweets to school, not doing PE and going to bed late. Ask the children what they think and if they would ever behave like that. Discuss their responses to Jenny's actions.

- Play 'Healthy or Unhealthy'. Make a selection of cards with pictures of healthy and unhealthy habits, such as, brushing your teeth, smoking, eating fruit, sleeping. Ask the children to sit in a circle and give each one a card. Place a green hoop for Unhealthy and a red hoop for Healthy in the centre. Play some gentle music and ask the children to place their card in the appropriate hoop, then discuss their choices.

- Play 'Healthy Habits' in pairs. Give each pair a whiteboard and a pen. On a spinner, write one aspect of a healthy lifestyle: 'exercise', 'rest', 'eating', and 'cleanliness' on each of four sections. Spin the spinner and ask the children to write down an appropriate healthy habit, for example, if it lands on 'exercise' the children could write 'play football', or for 'cleanliness', 'brush your teeth'.

Learning Objective

- To understand about factors that help us stay healthy and how to make healthy choices

Practical Activities

- Play 'Build a Healthy House', using a set of laminated boards in the shape of a house. Make a set of parts for each house, including a roof, door, windows, chimney. Place cards from the 'Healthy or Unhealthy' game (above) in a bag. Children take turns to pick a card. If they pick a healthy habit they add a part of their house. If they pick an unhealthy habit they must remove a part. The first child to build a complete house wins.

- Provide each child with a house-shaped booklet. Ask the children to draw different rooms in their house and examples of ways they and their family keep healthy. In the bathroom they might draw a picture of their brother or sister having a bubble bath, or in the kitchen, mum or dad cooking a healthy meal.

- Play 'Hunt for a Healthy Habit'. Gather a selection of around ten objects to represent healthy and unhealthy habits, for example, an apple, a trainer, a pillow, a bar of chocolate, a bottle of wine, a cigarette. Place the objects on a tray and let a small group of children have one minute to look at them. Cover the objects with a cloth and challenge the children to draw and write down as many healthy items as they can remember. An extension would be to remove one or two objects so the children have to identify which healthy habits are missing.

Art and Display

- Draw and use watercolour pencils to create a healthy house picture. The parts of the house must be made up of things representing healthy habits, such as, a toothbrush chimney, or a bubble bath window.

- For a class display, create a large house from collage materials. Colour mix different shades of red bricks. Finally, add labels showing healthy habits such as 'regular exercise'.

Cross-curricular Links

- **PE** – Set up circuit training sessions focusing on maintaining a healthy heart. Talk to the children about the importance of warming up and cooling down.

- **SCIENCE** – Discuss the effect of healthy and unhealthy habits on the body, for example, tooth decay.

- **MATHS** – Organise a survey to find out how healthy your school is. One group could survey how much exercise is carried out, another the type of snacks that are eaten.

Germ Catcher

Learning Objective

- To understand the importance of personal hygiene and for children to develop the skills to keep themselves clean

Whole-class Starter

- In role as the 'Germ Catcher' you enter the classroom dressed in a superhero-type costume with a large net. Inform the children that you are on the lookout for germs and ask them what a germ is and why they are allowed to exist on our planet. Ask the children where you might go to find germs. They may suggest places such as the toilet or kitchen. Tell the children that germs can be found on people and the only way to stop these germs from attacking and taking over the planet is to fight them with cleanliness.

- As the Germ Catcher, give each child a sticky note and ask them to write down or draw one way in which they can keep themselves clean and so fight germs, for example, 'I brush my teeth' or 'I comb my hair'. Collect up the notes in your germ-catching net. Discuss the children's responses with them.

Practical Activities

- Play 'Catch those Germs'. You need a fishing net, a set of balls or beanbags and a hoop. Each child takes a turn to stand in the hoop holding the germ-catching net. Throw one ball at a time in the air. If the child catches the ball, they must name a different way of fighting germs, for example, 'combing hair' or 'changing my clothes' to keep it. The child with the highest score wins.

- Play 'Beat the Germs' bingo. On a set of bingo boards put pictures or words that relate to unhygienic personal habits (make each board different). Make a dice with pictures or words relating to personal hygiene, for example, 'washing hands' or 'brushing teeth'. The children take turns to roll the dice and cover the corresponding germ on their board. So, if they roll 'washing hands' they would cover up 'just been to the toilet'. The first to get a line of three, wins.

- Produce a 'Goodbye to Germs' Guide Book. Ask the children to write down how they can say goodbye to germs by developing personal hygiene skills.

Art and Display

- Use paint and collage materials to create a giant 'Germ Catcher' superhero figure for display.

- Draw and paint pictures of things that help us keep clean, for example, a toothbrush, a washing machine or bubble bath.

- Paint and collage imaginary germs.

- Design a superhero. Label his characteristics, for example, 'sparkly, white teeth, brushed after every meal'.

Cross-curricular Links

- **SCIENCE** – Invite the school nurse to talk to the children about how to take care of their hair to prevent headlice.

  – Experiment to illustrate tooth decay and how it may be prevented. Give the children disclosing tablets to check for plaque on their teeth (parental permission needed). Reassure them that even the cleanest teeth will show up some plaque.

- **MUSIC** – Take the idea of *We're going on a Bear Hunt* by Michael Rosen (Walker Books) and introduce the children to a song called *We're going on a Germ Hunt*. Teach them the beginning of the song, then together they should write new verses relating to personal hygiene, and produce illustrations. It could start:

We're going on a Germ Hunt
We're going to find a nasty one
We're the hygiene gang
We're not scared!
Oh no, fingernails,
Dirty, grubby fingernails,
We can't ignore them,
We can't nibble them,
Oh no! We'll have to scrub them!
Scrub scrub swish! Scrub scrub swish!

As an alternative, create a rap about fighting germs.

Lazy Ozzie

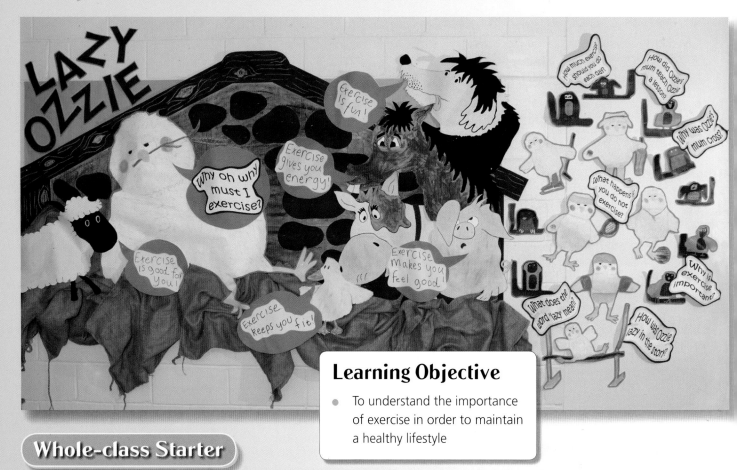

Learning Objective

- To understand the importance of exercise in order to maintain a healthy lifestyle

Whole-class Starter

- Read and enjoy *Lazy Ozzie* by Michael Coleman (Little Tiger Press). Discuss what the word 'lazy' means and why Ozzie was lazy in the story. Invite the children to discuss (in pairs) times when they might be lazy. Why are we lazy? What can we do to stop ourselves from being lazy? Why is it not good to be lazy?

- Lazy Ozzie arrives in the classroom (owl puppet). He is sad because his mum has told him off for being lazy. He is confused and does not know what she means. She keeps telling him that he must stop being lazy and exercise so he will get strong and learn to fly. He does not know what exercise means or how it can help him. He asks the children for help. They should volunteer ideas about exercise and why it is important.

- Ozzie asks the children what will happen to him when he exercises. Encourage the children to make suggestions about changes to Ozzie's body: his pulse will be faster, he will be breathless, he will sweat, his muscles will ache.

- Play 'Exercise your Alphabet'. Make a board with letters of the alphabet in order. Under each letter write 'L' (for left), 'R' (for right) or 'T' (for together). Let the children practise saying the alphabet, moving the corresponding arm(s). Children could then pick a letter and think of a form of exercise, such as 'F' for football, and spell the word using the board and arm actions. Challenge them to think of an activity for every letter.

Practical Activities

- Make an exercise alphabet. Ask the children to write and illustrate a form of exercise for each letter.

- Ask the children to keep a week's exercise diary. Encourage them to include every aspect of exercise they do, both in and out of school.

- Play 'Find My Fitness Level'. In small groups, ask the children to carry out certain exercises to discover their own level of fitness. These could include running twice around the playground, stepping on and off a low bench for three minutes, eight press ups or sit ups. Ask the children to use a five point scale to measure how hard they found each activity and record.

- Play 'Fitness for Fun' in a large space. In a small group, with children in teams of two, set up an obstacle course for each pair. Make a set of question cards about the effect of exercise on different parts of the body, such as: 'What does exercise do to your muscles?'; 'How does exercise affect your heart?' Make a set of corresponding answer cards: 'It makes them strong'; 'It increases your heart rate and makes it healthy'. Place an answer card at the end of each obstacle course. One child from each team races through the course, collects the answer card and races back. The teacher reads out a question and the team with the corresponding answer wins a point. The team with the most points wins.

Art and Display

- Use paint and collage materials to create a giant Lazy Ozzie, mummy owl and characters from the story for display.

- Chalk pastel pictures of Lazy Ozzie engaging in different sports.

- Make clay owls or use a plastic bottle and collage materials to fashion a 3D owl figure.
- Produce owl puppets from hessian, felt and feathers.

Why was Ozzie's mum cross?

Cross-curricular Links

- **PE** – Organise a mini Olympics or sports day.

- **ASSEMBLY** – Encourage the children to participate in 'Walk to School Week'.

- **LITERACY** – Create an acrostic of the word EXERCISE. Here is an example:

  Exercise
  Xtra effort makes you healthy
  Enjoy and achieve
  Race towards a healthy heart
  Continuous exercise keeps you fit
  It makes your heart beat faster
  So blood pumps around your body
  Everybody can exercise – just try!

- **ICT** – Using a data handling program, enter data on children's favourite form of exercise. Discuss the results.

Food Families

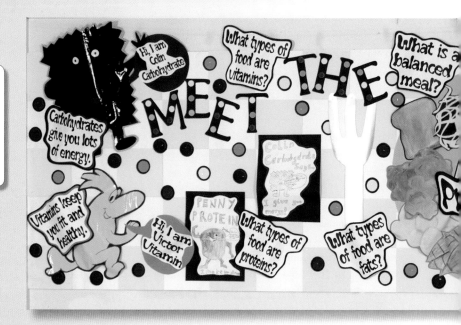

Whole-class Starter

- Make a set of puppets to represent characters from the different food families, for example, Penny Protein, Victor Vitamin, Colin Carbohydrate, Mary Mineral and Freddy Fat. The characters should be different colours, with features that correspond to their food group, for example, Penny Protein could have big muscles as proteins make you strong; Victor Vitamin could be green to symbolise fruit and vegetables. Introduce the puppets to the class and explain that they are your best friends because they keep you healthy. Explain why each character is important, what foods they are found in, and what that food group does for your body. Emphasise that they are all important for a balanced diet and a healthy lifestyle.

- Seat the children in a circle with five hoops in the middle. Place one of the food family puppets in each hoop. Give each child a piece of food and ask them to sort it into the correct hoop, so, for example, a carrot would be placed in Victor Vitamin's hoop.

- Play 'Food Family Facts'. Make a giant spinner with sections labelled: 'Carbohydrate', 'Protein', 'Vitamin', 'Fat' 'Mineral', and a star. Give each pair of children a whiteboard and a pen. Spin the spinner and challenge the children to write down an example of food from the family it points to, and how that food family helps them to keep healthy. If the spinner lands on 'Carbohydrate' the children might write 'bread' and 'it gives you energy'. If the spinner points to the star, the children must write down a food from each family to make a healthy meal.

- Play 'Make a Meal' in a large space. Choose five children as 'cooks' and give them all a chef's hat to wear. The remaining children need a laminated label showing one of the food family groups (ensure there are an equal number of each food family). On a signal, the children run around and try to avoid being caught by one of the chefs, while the chefs must try to catch and build a balanced meal with an ingredient from each food group. The first chef to 'cook' a balanced meal wins. An extension would be for the labels to show a laminated picture of a food item rather than a food family.

Practical Activities

- Play 'Healthy Habits'. Use the spinner from the 'Food Family Facts' game (above). Give each child in a small group a paper plate. They take turns to spin the spinner and to draw a picture of a food from the group indicated. The object is to create a balanced meal on their plate; if the spinner lands on the star, they add all their remaining ingredients.

- Design a Food Family poster that includes one of the characters with a speech bubble saying what they eat and how that helps them stay healthy.

- Take the children on a healthy hunt. Give each child in the group a chef's hat to wear, a whiteboard and a pen. Make a set of numbered plates depicting different meals, with one or two of the food families missing. Place the plates around the school or classroom. The children hunt for the plates, then identify which food is missing and write it on their whiteboard.

Art and Display

- Use paint and collage materials to create some large characters for display.

- Draw one of the food family characters. Cut out pictures of food corresponding to that character from magazines and use them to collage the character.

- Sculpt a balanced meal from clay or modelling material, or make a food family puppet.

- In groups of five, children draw and pastel a large piece of food from a different food family. They then arrange a balanced meal on a large colourful plate.

Cross-curricular Links

- **LITERACY** – Produce a 'Meet the Food Family' booklet, with a page for each food family character. Challenge the children to draw the character and write about foods where it can be found and why they are healthy.

- **SCIENCE** – Ask the children to keep a week's food diary. At the end of the week discuss whether or not they ate a balanced diet, and if they need to eat more from any particular food group(s).

- **DESIGN & TECHNOLOGY** – In small groups, plan, prepare and eat a balanced meal.

- **ROLE PLAY** – Create a café in which the children can practise making a balanced meal.

Peace at Last

Whole-class Starter

- Read and enjoy *Peace at Last* by Jill Murphy (Macmillan). Discuss the ways in which Mr Bear is kept awake and the effect this has on him.

- Ask the children to talk with a partner about the different things that might keep them awake at night. Encourage them to think about why it is important to get enough sleep and how they feel if they have slept badly.

- Mr Bear (you in role) visits the class in a really bad mood because he has not had enough sleep. The children should try to help Mr Bear by suggesting ways he could get a good night's rest, for example, earplugs or putting baby bear to bed earlier.

- Play 'Race to Bedtime'. Make two sets of cards, one set with suggestions of how to get to sleep, for example, 'a bedtime story with mummy or daddy', 'put your pyjamas on', 'go to bed when asked'. The second set shows suggestions of things that prevent you getting to sleep, such as, 'watch one more TV programme' or 'have a fizzy drink and a chocolate bar'. Place the cards in a bag. Divide the class into two teams in long lines. Give the child at the front of each line a teddy bear. The teams take turns to pick a card. If the card will help them get to sleep they roll a dice and move the teddy over and under the corresponding number of children. If the card prevents them going to sleep the teddy stays still. The first team to move their teddy all the way down the line wins.

Practical Activities

- Using pictures from the story ask the children to complete thought bubbles, suggesting ideas as to what Mr Bear is thinking and feeling.

- Produce a 'Do's and Don'ts' leaflet in which the children think up rules for getting a good night's sleep.

- Play 'Time for Bed, Mr Bear'. Make a set of board games in the shape of stairs, ending at Mr Bear's bed. On selected stairs write either things that will help Mr Bear get to sleep or things that will keep him awake. Give each child a board and a bear counter. The children take turns to roll the dice and travel upstairs to bed, obeying instructions along the way.

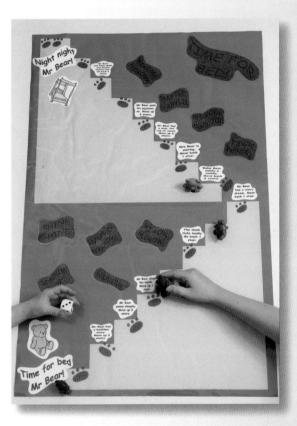

- Play 'What's the Time, Mr Bear?' in a large space. Make a set of cards showing things from the story that kept Mr Bear awake and an instruction, such as 'move three steps'. Make a second set of cards with a picture of Mr Bear asleep labelled 'Bedtime'. You need a mat, pillow and blanket for each player, plus a hoop and a bear mask. One child stands in the hoop wearing the bear mask at one end of the room as Mr Bear. The remaining children stand by their beds. On a signal the children ask, "What's the time, Mr Bear?". Mr Bear pulls out a card out and reads the instruction, for example, "Mrs Bear is snoring – move two steps forward". The children obey the instruction, moving towards Mr Bear. If Mr Bear pulls out a 'Bedtime' card the children race to their beds and get under the blanket. The last child in bed becomes Mr Bear and the game begins again.

Art and Display

- Use paint and collage materials to create a large Mr Bear display.

- Draw and chalk pastel pictures from the story of things that kept Mr Bear awake.

- Produce a Mr Bear mask from collage materials.

- Challenge children to make observational drawings of their own teddy bears.

Cross-curricular Links

- **DESIGN & TECHNOLOGY** – Design and make a bed for a teddy or Mr Bear.

- **LITERACY** – Draw a story map, mapping Mr Bear's dreadful night's sleep. Add thought bubbles indicating Mr Bear's thoughts and feelings.

- **MATHS** – Practise telling the time and the 24-hour clock.

What on Earth is a Human?

Whole-class Starter

Learning Objective

- To name the main parts of the body and identify the differences and similarities between people

- In role as an alien from another planet you enter the classroom and ask for help. You have been sent down to Earth to find out all about humans. Ask if anyone has seen a human anywhere. The children explain that they are humans but you reply that this cannot be true because they are not all alike. On your planet all aliens look exactly the same. Look at the children, pick out two and consider if they do look the same: they all have eyes, a head and hands. Appear confused and ask the children to help you understand how humans differ and how they are the same. Give each child two sticky notes and ask them to write on one something that is the same about all humans and on the other something that can be different. As a class, sort the notes into 'same' and 'different' lists and discuss.

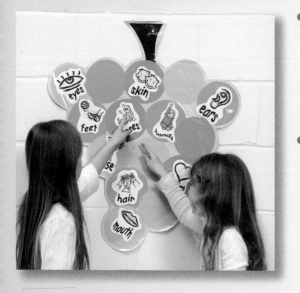

- Give each pair of children a whiteboard and a pen. Explain that you need to find out how humans are different so you can tell your alien friends. Make a set of cards with the names of body parts. Place them in a bag. Pull out a card and ask the children to write a list on their whiteboards of how this part of the human body might vary. For 'Hair' the children might write: 'long', 'short', 'black', 'blonde', 'curly' or 'straight'.

- Play 'Grapes'. Make a giant (A2) bunch of grapes, labelling each grape with a picture or word of a different body part: 'hair', 'eyes', 'skin' and so on. With the class in two teams, invite one member of each team to stand with their back to the grapes. Read out a clue, for example, 'the part of the body that helps you see', or 'can be blue, brown or green'. The two team members race to turn around and point to the correct grape first and score a point for their team. Repeat until every player has had a turn. The team with the most points wins.

Practical Activities

- Make a 'What on Earth is a Human?' booklet. Provide each child with a spiral-bound book with a picture of an alien on each page. Ask the children to draw a speech bubble and write a sentence describing how humans are the same in some ways but different in others, for example, 'Every human has a head, but humans have different coloured hair'.

- Play 'Build a Body'. Give each child an A4 piece of paper and a dice. In turn, roll a 1 or a 2 to start, then roll and draw according to the instructions: 1 for a head, 2 body, 3 legs, 4 arms, 5 facial features, 6 feet or hands. The first to complete their human wins.

- Play 'The Same but Different'. Give each child in a small group a folded zig-zag book in the shape of a person. Ask the children to start by drawing a person on the first page, pass their booklet on and draw a different person on the next page. Continue until all the pages are complete. Open up the booklet and reveal how many different kinds of human are depicted.

- Tell the children that the alien has invited them to visit his planet but they need a passport to go. Suggest they make their own. They must include all their identifying distinguishing features, including eye and hair colour.

Art and Display

- Use paint and collage materials to create a giant alien or giant human (or both) for display. Paint a variety of different aliens.

- Have a 'Mad Hair Day' and ask the children to design crazy hairstyles.

- Make human puppets with moving body parts.

- Produce clay sculptures of human beings.

Cross-curricular Links

- **DESIGN & TECHNOLOGY** – Design and make an alien using reclaimed materials.

- **MATHS** – Challenge the children to gather data about hair and eye colour and create bar or block graphs to show results. Discuss the outcomes to find what is the most common eye or hair colour.

- **SCIENCE** – Draw and label parts of the body and their functions.

Look out, Patrick!

Whole-class Starter

- Read and enjoy *Look out, Patrick!* by Paul Geraghty (Red Fox). Discuss the possible dangers Patrick encountered on his journey and other potential dangers that the children may encounter at home.

- Play 'Spin a Danger'. Give each pair of children a whiteboard and a pen. Label a spinner with the names of different rooms in the house, such as, 'bathroom', 'kitchen', 'hallway'. Spin the spinner and encourage the children to discuss and write down a potential danger that may occur in the room it lands on.

- Play 'I Spy a Danger'. Make a selection of A3 pictures of different rooms in the house. Include some showing a potential danger, on others make the rooms completely safe. Give each child a green card for safety and a red card for danger. Show the children one picture at a time and ask them to 'I spy' any dangers. If they can spy a danger they hold up their red card if not, they choose the green one. Discuss their decisions and ask the children how the danger could be avoided.

Learning Objective

- To understand potential dangers in the home and how to keep safe from these dangers

Practical Activities

- Ask the children to draw and colour a picture of a room in their house, showing at least ten dangers. Laminate the pictures. Give the children whiteboard pens; ask them to study a friend's picture and try to identify the ten possible dangers.

- Make a large selection of A4 laminated pictures of dangers you find in the home, such as, toys on the stairs, boiling water in a pan, hot iron, plastic carrier bags, open bottle of pills. Ask the children to sort the pictures using their own criteria. Repeat the exercise several times using different criteria. Suggestions are: by room; by type of danger (choking, burning); by level of danger (life threatening). Discuss which dangers they might solve themselves and which they must report to an adult.

- Play 'Danger Mouse' by making a board game based on *Look out, Patrick!* Prepare a set of scenario cards showing potential dangers in the home: 'You see a pan boiling on the stove and tell your mum straight away – move forward three spaces' or maybe 'You see your baby brother playing with a plastic bag but ignore him and carry on watching TV – miss a go'. Create a board with a route showing potential dangers and a counter. If the player encounters a danger they must pick up a scenario card and follow the instructions.

- Play 'House of Hazards'. Make bingo boards (one per child) in the shape of a house. On each square draw a potential danger in the home. Make a set of solution cards to the dangers. Place the cards around a large space. To the accompaniment of the *Mission Impossible* theme tune, the children must collect six solution cards that they think match their board. When the music stops ask the children to match the solutions to their boards; the first to complete their board shouts, "I've got a safe house".

Art and Display

- Use paint and collage materials to create a large class display to illustrate the *Look Out, Patrick!* story. Add labels to help children become aware of potential dangers.

- Draw and paint giant safety symbols.

Cross-curricular Links

- **GEOGRAPHY** – Draw an imaginary map of Patrick's journey.

- **ICT** – Use a programmable toy as Patrick and invite the children to follow a route avoiding dangers on the way.

- **LITERACY** – Make a collection of danger captions and look for danger words in the environment, such as, 'Beware', 'Danger', 'Hazard' and 'Look out'.

The Huge Bag of Worries

Whole-class Starter

- Read and enjoy *The Huge Bag of Worries* by Virginia Ironside (Hodder Children's Books). Discuss with the children the types of worries they have at school. Ask them to think about different aspects of the school day and any worries they may have in relation to this part of the day, such as, playtime, PE or going to the toilet.

- As a class, brainstorm the network of people within school who can help with any worries or problems children might have, from tiny worries, like losing a jumper to a big worry, for example, an older child behaving inappropriately towards a younger one.

- Play 'Solve your Worries'. Place eight mats around a large space, labelled with names of different people within the school support network: 'Headteacher', 'office staff', 'lunch supervisor', 'book buddy', 'friend' and so forth. Make a set of scenario cards relating to particular worries children might have. Read out a scenario and let the children decide which support person could help them, then run and sit on that mat. Discuss the children's responses. The music *Don't Worry, Be Happy* by Bobby McFerrin could be played.

Learning Objective

- To understand how to develop strategies to deal with personal problems or worries at school in order to ensure that we keep safe

Practical Activities

- Ask the children to draw a network map indicating the people they personally would turn to with a problem or worry. This could be extended by suggesting they give an example of how this person might help, for example, 'I would go to my big sister if I lost my friends on the playground'.

- Play 'The Huge Bag of Worries'. Make a set of bag-shaped laminated boards (one per child in the group). Make a spinner of members of the school network team. Ask each child in the group to write or draw six worries on sticky notes and place them on their board. Each child takes a turn to spin the spinner. They must decide if that person could help them to solve any of their worries. If they can, the child removes the worry from their bag and pops it in the bin. The object is to remove all their worries.

- In a drama session, with children in small groups, give each group a scenario card from the 'Solve your Worries' game (see page 20). Challenge them to role-play the problem and a possible solution. Ask each group to perform their scenario at the end of the session for the other children to watch and discuss.

- Play 'Work out your Worries'. Get a set of small drawstring bags (one per child in the group) and sit the children in a circle. Ask them to write a worry they might have at school on a piece of paper and put it in their bag. They then pass the bags around the circle while singing to the tune of *London Bridge is Falling Down*:

Pass the bag around the ring, around the ring, around the ring,
Pass the bag around the ring,
Work out your worries!

When the song stops, spin a bottle and the child indicated should read the worry in the bag they are holding and offer a solution.

Art and Display

- Use paint and collage materials to create a picture of a girl from the story and a huge bag of worries.

- Paint and collage pictures of people from your school network.

Cross-curricular Links

- **ASSEMBLY** – Create a school Worry Box to leave in a central place and encourage the children to deposit their worries there. Ask the school council to discuss the worries and offer solutions and help.

- **DANCE** – Using suitable music, such as *Lean on Me* by Bill Withers, create a dance to illustrate the idea of supporting each other with an emphasis on balance.

- **LITERACY** – Write a poem about worries with contrasting lines. Here is an example:

Standing alone in the corner of the playground,
Isolated no-one to play with but the shadow,
Hesitantly I ask to join the game,
Smiles surround me and we skip off together,
I can lean on friends who rescue me from the shadows.

Beware of the Big Bad Wolf

Learning Objective

● To understand the rules for, and ways of, keeping ourselves safe

Whole-class Starter

● Read or retell the classic fairy tale, *Little Red Riding Hood*. Discuss the parts in the story when Little Red Riding Hood was in danger. Who was she in danger from? How was she in danger? What could she have done differently to keep herself safe?

● In role as Little Red Riding Hood, visit the class in a bit of a panic. Explain you got lost on your way to Granny's house when you saw some lovely flowers to pick and wandered off the path, and then heard some music and followed the sound. Start to cry, saying, "I don't know what to do". Children should explain that you should have followed your mum's instructions and tell you how to keep safe from now on. Give each pair of children a large laminated apple and ask them to write a rule that will help keep Little Red Riding Hood safe in future. They might write: 'never talk to a stranger'; 'only talk to someone you can trust' or 'don't walk anywhere on your own'. Little Red Riding Hood puts the apples in her bag and makes her way home safely.

● Play 'Stranger Danger'. Make a set of cards depicting different people, such as, mummy, police officer, stranger in a car, ice-cream man, crossing patrol officer and a lady on a bench. Give each child a card. Play some gentle music and ask the children to sort the cards into two hoops, one labelled 'Beware – Stranger Danger!' and the other, 'Safe and Sound'.

● Discuss with the class places they go when not at school. Where do they go with their family? With their friends? On their own? Responses could include: 'swimming pool', 'cinema', 'park'. Write these places on the board. In pairs, ask the children to write or draw on a sticky note a safety rule for one place and stick it on the board, for example, 'Stay with your friends at the park'.

Practical Activities

● Play 'Safe and Sound'. Make a large board game portraying Little Red Riding Hood's journey to Granny's cottage. The children must move along the board towards the safety of the house. However, along the way are scenarios for Little Red Riding Hood to deal with, for example, 'Big Bad Wolf talks to you and you say "hello". Move back five spaces.' The first player to arrive safely wins.

- Make a 'Stranger Danger' leaflet or poster illustrating what to do if a stranger approaches you. Discuss with the children positive things they can do to keep safe and include these on their poster. You could also invite a local police officer into school to talk to the children about 'Stranger Danger'.

- Play 'Deal with a Danger'. Make two sets of laminated cards: one set red and spiky cards with real-life danger scenarios, for example, 'you lose your friends in the park'; the second set show responses to a danger scenario: 'find a policeman'; 'find a telephone and phone home'; 'accept a lift home from a stranger'. Children select a danger card and then a response card. If the response solves the danger safely they keep the cards, if the response puts them in danger, they put the cards back.

- Discuss with a group the importance of learning their personal information as a way of keeping them safe. Make small identity cards with their name, address and telephone number. Talk about the importance of not sharing personal details with strangers.

Art and Display

- Use paint and collage materials to create a giant Big Bad Wolf and Little Red Riding Hood display.

- Design and draw giant safety symbols relevant to different places.

- Make Little Red Riding Hood and Wolf Puppets for role-playing activities.

- Make giant 'Stranger Danger Flowers' from wood and card, with a safety rule on each petal. These could be displayed in flowerpots around the school.

Cross-curricular Links

- **GEOGRAPHY** – Draw an imaginary map of Little Red Riding Hood's journey to Granny's cottage.

- **ICT** – Dress a programmable toy as Little Red Riding Hood. Program it to follow a route to Granny's cottage.

- **DRAMA** – Ask children to imagine what would have happened if Little Red Riding Hood had kept herself safe from danger. Invent a new story and act it out.

999 Help!

Whole-class Starter

- A police officer (you in role) arrives in class and expresses concern that when people telephone the emergency services they often do not know which service they need. Ask the children for their help. Talk to them about all the emergency services and how they keep us safe.

- Play 'Dial 999'. Give each pair of children a whiteboard and a pen. Read out a scenario for the children to discuss and decide whether or not it is an emergency. If yes, they write '999' on their whiteboards, if not they write 'tell an adult'.

- Play 'Spin a Service' with the children sitting in a circle around a selection of props and costumes relating to the emergency services. Read out a scenario and spin a bottle. The child indicated dresses up in an appropriate costume and explains what they would do.

- Play 'Search for a Service'. Make two sets of cards, one set showing a problem, for example, a cat up a tree, the second depicting an emergency service. Give each child a card and on a signal they have to find their partner.

Practical Activities

- Play '999 Bingo', using a set of bingo boards with pictures of emergency services and suitable scenario cards. In turn, the children pick a scenario card out of a bag and cover the appropriate emergency service on their board. You could also include '999' cards. If a child picks a '999' card the rest of the group must uncover one of their emergency service pictures.

Learning Objective

- To understand that people can help keep us safe

- Play '999 I Need Help' with a set of suitable scenario cards and two toy telephones. In pairs, the children pick out a scenario card. One child should act as the emergency service, the other the caller, while they conduct an appropriate conversation.

- Make 'I spy' books, one per child, with a peephole at the centre of each page. The children write a scenario and ask the question, 'Which emergency service can you spy?'. Behind the peephole they draw a picture of the correct emergency service.

- Invite representatives from a range of emergency services into school to talk to the children. Alternatively, arrange a visit to a fire station, police station or hospital. Afterwards, display a large picture of an emergency service worker.

Art and Display

- Ask children to paint a self-portrait as a member of an emergency service, then to write the characteristics they think they would need around it.

- Use paint and collage materials to create large images of members of the emergency services for display.

- Draw large 999 numbers and invite the children to fill them with pictures relating to the emergency services.

Cross-curricular Links

- **DESIGN & TECHNOLOGY** – Design and make an emergency service vehicle.

- **SCIENCE** – Help Fireman Fred light the bulb on his fire engine (focus on electrical circuits).

- **DRAMA** – Turn the role-play area into a fire station, police station or hospital.

Rules of the Road

Learning Objective

- To understand the dangers that may exist on the road and how to keep safe when crossing or playing near the road

Whole-class Starter

- Tell the children that the school has received a letter from the Local Authority informing them that due to insufficient funds there will no longer be a Crossing Patrol Officer. Just the flashing warning lights will alert motorists to the presence of schoolchildren. Appalled by what is happening, ask the children what they can do to make sure they are safe when crossing the road. Discuss the dangers they face crossing the road and strategies they can use to keep safe. Invite the Crossing Patrol Officer into school to talk to the children. Encourage the children to ask questions about road safety.

- Discuss with the children what they should think about when crossing the road. Give each pair of children a whiteboard and a pen and ask them to write down what they should do when crossing any road, for example, 'Stop', 'Look', 'Listen' and 'Cross'. Ask the children to think of actions they could do to represent the words. For example, 'Stop' – raise one hand, 'Look' – point to eyes, 'Listen' – point to ears and 'Cross' – make a cross shape with hands or arms.

- Discuss the dangers of cars and their speed. Ask the children to think of ideas to slow down traffic. In groups of three or four, ask them to think of a slogan that will either help combat fast traffic or encourage pedestrians to cross with care. For example, 'Be a tortoise and drive s-l-o-w-l-y'. Ask each group to write their slogan on a long piece of card. Cut the cards in half and place face down on the carpet. The children sit in a circle and take turns to pick up two pieces of card. If they make a safety slogan they stick it on the board, if they do not match they replace them and the next child takes their turn.

Practical Activities

- Ask the children to reply to the Local Authority and explain how they will help the children in the school become road safety conscious. Encourage them to write about dangers and how they will help their classmates stay safe when playing by or crossing the road.

- Recreate a road situation in the school playground. Ask the children to practise crossing the road safely. If possible, transfer this to a road close to the school (you will need parental permission for this activity).

- Ask the children to write a leaflet for younger children to help them cross the road safely.

- Play 'Cross the Road Safely'. Make large cards that can be attached to a child's clothing. Write one word on each: 'Stop', 'Look', 'Listen' or 'Cross'. Give each child in the group a card to wear except one who must be the Green Cross Code Man and wear a green bib. Cone off an allocated area; ask the children to stand at one end and the Green Cross Code Man in the middle. On a signal such, as "cross the road safely" the children try to cross the area, while the Green Cross Code Man tries to tag them. However he must tag them in the correct order: 'Stop' first, then 'Look', 'Listen' and 'Cross'. Tagged children are out of the game and must stand still. Once all four have been tagged another child becomes the Green Cross Code Man.

Art and Display

- Use paint and collage materials to create a large crossing patrol officer and cars for the display.

- Paint large road signs, cars and slogans from the whole-class starter.

- Create an eye-catching poster to remind children always to stop, look and listen before crossing the road.

Cross-curricular Links

- **MATHS** – Carry out a road safety survey to discover volume of traffic and busy times of the day.

- **GEOGRAPHY** – Draw a route to school and identify the roads children have to cross and where they might cross them safely.

- **DESIGN & TECHNOLOGY** – Design and make a reflective item that can be used to keep children safe in the dark.

Rules Rule!

Whole-class Starter

- Retell the story of *The Sorcerer's Apprentice* by Inga Moore (Walker Books) using visual aids and props from the story, such as a broomstick, a bucket, a sorcerer's cape and a hat. Discuss what the apprentice did that was wrong and the consequences of his behaviour. Talk about what a rule is, why we have rules and what would happen if we did not have any.

- Encourage the children to discuss with a partner an occasion when they have broken a rule and what happened as a result. Ask them to share their experiences with the class.

- Give each child a whiteboard and a pen. Challenge the children to write as many school rules as they can think of in one minute. Ask them to write one school rule on a sticky note. Label four sheets of paper with different types of school rules, such as: 'playtime rules', 'classroom rules', 'lunchtime rules', 'whole school rules'. Invite the children to stick their rule under the appropriate title. Discuss who is responsible for ensuring these rules are carried out.

- Play 'Roll a Rule' by placing the sticky notes (as above) on the board. Discuss different types of rules – those that keep us safe and those that help us behave. Make a dice, marked 'safety' on three faces and 'behaviour' on three. The children sit in a circle around two hoops, with the same labels, then take turns to roll the dice. If it lands on 'safety' they choose a safety rule from the board to place in the 'safety' hoop, for example, 'Don't run in school'. If it lands on 'behaviour' they choose a behaviour rule, for example, 'Listen carefully on the carpet'.

Learning Objective

- To understand the importance of rules and the reasons for different rules

Practical Activities

- Play 'Rules Rule' in a large space. You need: four benches, four hoops, a large bucket, a hooter and a gong. Make a set of laminated cards of school rules, another set showing school rules that have been broken, plus a set depicting a broomstick or a sorcerer's hat. Place the cards in the bucket in the middle of the area. Split the children into four groups and set up a small obstacle course for each group using the benches and hoops. On a signal from the hooter a child from each team races to the bucket, going across the bench and through the hoop, collects a card and returns to the group. Together they read the card and decide what to do. If it is a school rule they keep the card and the next person takes their turn. If it is a broken rule they bang the gong and the game stops. As a group they discuss how they could prevent the rule from being broken. Once they have given the explanation they keep the card and the game continues. A broomstick or sorcerer's hat card means they must put all their rules back in the bucket.

- Ask the children to create a 'Remember the Rules' poster or banner. Encourage them to think about the importance of rules and why we need them.

- Play 'Round up your Rules'. Make three different sets of laminated cards in three different colours (blue, green, pink). On the green set write rules that are familiar to the children, for example, 'Do not run around the school'. On the pink set write the reason: 'You might slip over or run into someone'. On the blue set write the type of rule: 'I am a safety rule'. Place the cards face down; the children take turns to pick up three cards, one of each colour. If they get a full set they keep the cards. The object is to collect as many sets as possible.

Art and Display

- Use paint and collage materials to create a class sorcerer's apprentice display. Paint large broomsticks and colour mix shades of blue on water droplet-shaped pieces of paper.

- Ask the children to think of a school rule to illustrate to be displayed around the school or classroom.

Cross-curricular Links

- **ASSEMBLY** – As a whole school, discuss the importance of rules and why we need them. Create a set of 'Golden Rules' to be used as guidelines for general school behaviour.

- **DRAMA** – In small groups, using props from the story, invite the children to re-enact the story of *The Sorcerer's Apprentice*. Challenge them to think of an alternative ending.

- **HISTORY** – Discuss school rules from the past. How do they compare to today's rules? Talk about the consequences of breaking rules, compared with today. Think about Victorian rules.

George's Marvellous Medicine

Whole-class Starter

- Read *George's Marvellous Medicine* by Roald Dahl (Puffin). Focus on chapters 2, 3 and 4 when George makes the potion for his grandmother. Discuss how George's concoction had disastrous consequences because it was not a real medicine. Talk about what medicines are and why we need them.

- Play 'Bathroom Bonanza'. Collect an assortment of products and medicines found in the bathroom, such as, toothpaste, shampoo and headache tablets. With the children sitting in a circle, give everyone an item to sort into two hoops, according to whether it is a medicine or not. Discuss their choices, the difference between the two hoops and the fact that medicines should be kept in a locked cupboard for safety.

- Jasmin (you in role) enters, clutching a handful of pills that you have found in mum's bathroom cabinet. Explain that you are excited to have found all these sweeties in the bathroom and no-one knows you have them. Say you offered to share them with your best friend but that she said 'no thanks' and told Jasmin she was silly. Tell the children you were not being silly, but kind and suggest they might like to share the sweets. Encourage the children to explain to you the danger of your actions and what to do now. Ask them to help you remember by writing a set of safety rules to take home on large laminated 'medicine' bottles. They could suggest: 'Only take medicine that a trusted adult has given you'; 'Do not take anyone else's medicine'; 'Only take the correct amount of medicine'; 'Make sure medicines are put back in a safe place'.

Learning Objective

- To recognise the role of medicine; to understand that all medicines are drugs, and what their benefits and dangers might be

Practical Activities

- In a small group, examine a selection of medicine packets and bottles. Discuss what the different medicines are for, where you would find instructions for taking the medicine, any safety advice, and the kind of medicines they are.

- Play 'Pick the Pill' in a group with adult supervision. Make ten cards, numbered 1–10, with either a 'pill' or a sweet stuck in the centre. Give each child a laminated answer sheet with 1–10 down the side and a pen. Present the children with one of the cards to pass around the group to study closely, then decide whether the 'pill' is a medicine or a sweet and write the appropriate word next to the number on their board. At the end, the children discuss their responses and you reveal the correct answers.

- Ask the children to design posters that can be displayed around the school about keeping medicines safe and the dangers of medicines.

- Invite the school nurse or local doctor into school to talk to the children about the importance of medicine, its benefits and potential dangers.

Art and Display

- Create a large picture of George from the story using collage materials.

  - Ask the children to draw from close observation a range of medicine packets and bottles.

    - Design and make a cuboid medicine packet to place in a class bathroom cabinet.

Cross-curricular Links

- **LITERACY** – Taking inspiration from *George's Marvellous Medicine*, ask the children to write their own naughty potion recipe on medicine bottle shapes. Collect them into a class book.

- **MATHS** – Discuss the shapes of medicine bottles and packets with the children as a starter for 3D shape work.

- **SCIENCE** – Investigate what 'soluble' means and carry out experiments to investigate substances that dissolve.

Horrid Henry

Whole-class Starter

Learning Objective

● To understand the consequences of breaking rules within the family, and the importance of keeping these rules

● Read and discuss the story *Horrid Henry* by Francesca Simon (Orion). Ask the children to brainstorm with a partner the different ways that Henry broke the rules. Discuss the consequences of Henry's behaviour as a class. How does it affect his family life? Have they ever broken a rule at home? What were the consequences? How did they feel about breaking the rules? Did anyone find out? What was their punishment?

● In role as Horrid Henry, talk to the children about how you love to break rules at home and cannot understand the need for rules. Tell them how last night you broke the rule about going to bed at eight o'clock and played computer games until late, so your parents have taken the computer away for a week. Why do parents love making up rules? Ask the class if their parents make up rules at home. Give each child a sticky note and ask them to write down or draw a rule in their house. Collect them up and discuss why these rules are necessary and what happens if they are broken.

● Play 'Reasons for Rules'. Make three sets of cards on three different colours: one set with rules, for example, 'Don't talk with your mouth full'; another with reasons: 'It's not nice to look at chewed-up food in someone's mouth'; and the third showing a sanction, such as 'You are told to leave the table'. Give each child a card. Play some gentle music and ask the children to move around the classroom and, without talking, to complete their set of cards. Ask them to explain their set to see if it makes sense.

● Play 'Rules or Rubbish?' with two sets of cards of the same colour. One set should show real examples of family rules, such as, 'Go to bed when your parents tell you'. The other set shows 'nonsense rules', for example, 'You must eat breakfast standing on your head'. Deal out the cards (one each) to children standing in a circle. Go around the circle and reveal one child's card at a time. If the child has a real rule they stay in the game, if they have a nonsense rule they are eliminated and sit down. Repeat until all the cards have been used.

Practical Activities

- Ask the children to be 'Rule-makers' and to consider rules for their family, related to their bedroom. They might suggest: 'Knock before you come in'; 'If you borrow a book put it back on the shelf'; 'Toys belong in the green box'. Ask the children to design and colour a 'Bedroom Code of Behaviour' to display on their bedroom door.

- Play 'Roll for Rules' with a set of A3 bingo boards. On each square write a different rule relating to family life. Ensure you include a mix of: safety rules (Never take anything electrical into the bathroom); behaviour rules (Don't slam doors); relationship rules (Don't pinch your sister) and hygiene rules (Brush your teeth before bed). Label a set of skittles: Safety, Behaviour, Relationship and Hygiene, and on two skittles stick a picture of Horrid Henry. The children should roll a ball and knock over as many skittles as they can, avoiding Horrid Henry. For each skittle they knock down they cover a corresponding rule on their board. If they knock down Horrid Henry they must uncover all their rules and start again. The first person to cover all their squares wins.

- Play 'Rules Snap'. Give each child eight square pieces of card and ask them to write and illustrate four different family rules and the four reasons for those rules. Laminate and play within the class.

Art and Display

- Use paint and collage materials to create a large Horrid Henry display.

- Ask the children to draw and paint their own Horrid Henry picture and around it to write reasons why rules should not be broken.

- Draw a picture of a family member and around the edge write sentences about the rules they are responsible for enforcing, for example, 'Dad makes me brush my teeth after every meal'.

Cross-curricular Links

- **LITERACY** – Ask the children to draw their own cartoon strip based on a *Horrid Henry* story by Francesca Simon or challenge them to write their own Horrid Henry episode.

- **HISTORY** – Introduce family rules from the past, such as, 'Children should be seen and not heard'. Discuss the consequences of this saying, how rules have changed and why.

Helping Hands

Learning Objective

- To understand what it means to be helpful and different ways to help others

Whole-class Starter

- Bring into class a large box of objects and tell the children that you have been having a clear-out at home and found all of these things that should be in school. Can the children help to put them back where they belong? Emphasise how helpful the children are being as they return the objects to their rightful places. Discuss why it is important to be helpful.

- Brainstorm together everything that children do at school to be helpful, such as, tidying the book corner and their tables, washing cups at snack time, returning the register.

- Give each pair of children a large laminated hand shape and a whiteboard pen. Ask them to draw a picture or write a sentence about somebody they help at school and how, for example, 'I help my friend put her socks on after PE'. This activity can be repeated for helping at home, for example, 'I help my dog keep fit by taking it for a walk'.

- Play 'Hunt for Help'. Make a set of laminated hands (one per child). Each hand should have a letter from the word 'help'. Play *Help* by The Beatles while the children walk around the classroom and, without talking, find the letters to spell 'help'. Then they must sit down with their group and discuss together one way of being helpful. The children could share their ideas with the rest of the class.

Practical Activities

- Give each child a hand-shaped piece of paper (larger than A4). Ask them to draw a picture of someone they help on each fingernail and write how they help them along each finger.

- Play 'Helping Hands'. Make card pairs of hands in two colours. On one colour write a problem that needs help to resolve, for example, 'There are toys on the stairs'. On the other, write a way of helping that would solve the problem, for example, 'Put the toys in the toy box'. The children take turns to turn over two different coloured cards. If they match they keep them, if not they return them face down. The child with most pairs at the end wins.

- Play 'Hurry to be Helpful'. Hang lots of pairs of rubber gloves on a washing line in a large space. Make a set of scenario cards, presenting problems for the children to help to resolve, such as, 'Baby brother is crying and mummy is on the phone'. Make a set of forfeit cards, for example, 'Put all your gloves back', 'Miss a turn' or 'Have an extra turn'. With children in two teams, each team takes turns to pick a card from a bag. If it is a scenario card they must discuss as a group how they could be helpful and solve the problem. If their answer is helpful, they run and get a rubber glove for one member of their team to wear. If they pick a forfeit card they must follow the instructions. The object is for each child in the team to wear a pair of rubber gloves!

- Give each group of two or three children a different scenario to mime, for example, 'A younger child on the playground has dropped his snack'. The children must mime the problem and a possible way that they could help. The rest of the class must try and guess what has happened.

Art and Display

- Make 'Helping Hand' pictures. Ask the children to make a print of their own hand and turn it into a picture. Alternatively, they could print multiple hands onto an A3 sheet to be cut out and made into a giant image for display, such as a hedgehog or tree.

- Produce clay hands by cutting around children's own hands on a clay tile and use clay tools to sculpt the features of their hand.

- Ask children to oil pastel a pair of gloves and arrange them to make a whole class helping hands collage.

Cross-curricular Links

- **LITERACY** – Work on adjectives to describe the children's gloves. Ask them to bring in a pair of gloves from home: rubber gloves, baby's mittens, driving gloves, gardening gloves, even boxing gloves. Think of a range of adjectives to describe the different gloves, for example, 'Helping hands are leather hands'.

- **MATHS** – Work on pairs, for example, sorting gloves and counting in twos.

- **SCIENCE** – Challenge the children to draw a hand, then to label its parts and their functions.

The Rainbow Fish

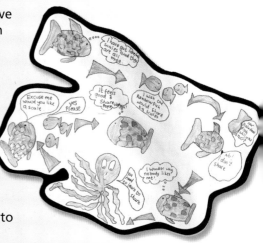

Whole-class Starter

- Read and enjoy *The Rainbow Fish* by Marcus Pfister (North-South Books). Discuss how the Rainbow Fish changed throughout the story. Ask the children what made the Rainbow Fish change. How did the Rainbow Fish feel once he shared his scales? Give each child a sticky note to write down why it is important to share. Discuss their responses.

- Talk about different ways of sharing and the effect it has on our lives. Give each pair of children a whiteboard and a pen. Make a set of rainbow fish with one letter from the word 'share' on each fish.
Place the fish in a blue bag. Pick out a letter and ask the children to discuss with their partner a phrase or word beginning with the letter that relates to how and why we share. The letter 'S' could prompt the phrase 'Sharing is caring' or the letter 'E', 'Everybody needs to share'.

- Discuss how a major part of sharing is being cooperative and working as a team. Play the team game 'Swim Fishy Swim'. Make a set of large letters that spell out the word 'share' and place them around a big area. Make a set of large paper fish, plus a set of fish 'wafters' from rolled up newspaper. Make a set of cards showing the word 'share' with a different letter missing on each one. Split the class into

Learning Objective

- To understand the importance of sharing and that sharing is an essential part of citizenship

five groups and give each group a paper fish and a wafter. Show the class a card with a letter missing. They then 'waft' their fish as quickly as they can to the missing letter. The first team to arrive scores a point.

Practical Activities

- Make a zig-zag 'Sharing Caring' book. On each page ask the children to write and illustrate the types of things we can share and the people we can share them with. They might write: 'Share a smile with a friend'; 'Share a hug with your mum'; 'Share some sweets with your brother'. This could be made into a large A3 class book.

- Play 'Fish for Thought'. Make a set of laminated fish with kind and unkind words written on them. Place the fish in a paddling pool. The children take turns to hook out a fish with a net. If they catch a fish with a kind word on they use the word to make a sentence. If they catch a fish with an unkind word on they throw it away.

- Ask the children to draw a story map depicting the main event in the story and to add speech or thought bubbles to show how the Rainbow Fish and other fish changed throughout the story.

Art and Display

- Use paint and collage materials to create a large Rainbow Fish, octopus and smaller fish for display. Add labels giving examples of sharing, such as, 'I share toys with my brother'.

- Ask the children to sew a Rainbow Fish, using hessian, felt, silver fabric and thread. Alternatively, practise a weaving technique and weave the scales of the Rainbow Fish.

- Using a paper tearing technique, ask the children to make several fish and arrange on a marbled background.

- Give the children a variety of tools and challenge them to print a fish with scales, waves and seaweed as part of an underwater scene.

Cross-curricular Links

- **DESIGN & TECHNOLOGY** – Make a concertina Rainbow Fish using a paper folding technique.

- **DRAMA** – With children working in small groups, allow them to retell *The Rainbow Fish* by Marcus Pfister in their own way.

- **RE** – Introduce stories that highlight the importance of sharing, for example, the Christian story of *The Feeding of the Five Thousand* from *My Own Book of Bible Stories* by Pat Alexander (Lion). Discuss the actions of the little boy and how Jesus and his disciples reacted to the boy's actions.

The Smartest Giant

Whole-class Starter

- Read and enjoy *The Smartest Giant in Town* by Julia Donaldson (Macmillan), but stop before the end, where the giant is upset because he has given away all his clothes. Discuss the ways in which the giant helped others in the story and how that makes him a good citizen.

- Discuss the concept of citizenship and what makes a good citizen. Spell 'citizenship' in giant letters and, with children in threes, give each team a letter and ask them to think of a phrase explaining how to be a good citizen beginning with that letter. As a class put the phrases together to make an acrostic poem of 'citizenship'.

Practical Activities

- Play 'Dress the Giant'. Give each child a board with a picture of the giant in his underwear, plus a set of laminated clothes that can be stuck onto the giant. Produce a set of scenario cards, for example, 'You spot someone in your class sitting on their own in the playground' and a spinner alternating 'I'm a good citizen' with sad faces. Put the scenario cards in a bag. The children take turns to pick a card and spin the spinner. If it lands on 'I'm a good citizen' they must think of a way to be a good citizen and solve the problem so they can add a piece of clothing to their giant. If they spin a sad face they miss a turn. The first player to dress their giant wins.

Learning Objective

- Understanding the meaning of citizenship and how to be a good citizen

- Give each child a piece of A3 paper in the shape of a giant tie for them to illustrate with a picture and caption showing how they could be a good citizen. At the top write 'Tie to be a Good Citizen!'.

- Children write a letter to the giant thanking him for teaching them to be good citizens. Encourage them to write about ways they might demonstrate citizenship in their own lives.

- Ask the children to draw a self-portrait wearing their favourite clothes. On each item of clothing they should write a way in which this item of clothing might help somebody, for example, 'My jumper could be an extra blanket for my baby brother'.

Art and Display

- Use paint and collage materials to create a large giant for display. Add labels showing good citizenship qualities.

- Paint characters from the story.

- Use oil pastels to design bold patterns on giant ties.

Cross-curricular Links

- **ASSEMBLY** – Introduce a weekly 'Citizenship' award. One child from the school is selected every week by the staff as an exemplary citizen and is presented with an award.

- **LITERACY** – Play rhyming games based around the rhyming words in the story.

- **RE** – Read and discuss the Christian story of *The Good Samaritan* from *My Own Book of Bible Stories* by Pat Alexander (Lion). Ask the children to compare it with the story of the giant.

- **GEOGRAPHY** – Draw a map of the giant's journey and include geographical words such as river, path and village.

The Enormous Turnip

Learning Objective

- To understand the importance of cooperating with others in order to work as a team

Whole-class Starter

- In role as a farmer retell the story of *The Enormous Turnip*. Explain to the children that you do not understand how a tiny mouse managed to pull out the turnip – he must be the strongest mouse in the world! How can a mouse be stronger than all the people in the story? Ask the children what they think. Encourage them to explain that the turnip came out not because the mouse was particularly strong but because everybody worked together. They all cooperated and worked as a team which made them stronger.

- Talk about what 'cooperate' means. Give each pair of children a turnip-shaped laminated card and ask them to discuss and write down an example of how they cooperate at school, at home or in the wider community. Discuss their responses, emphasising the importance of cooperation and the benefits it brings.

- Introduce the phrases: 'There is no "I" in team', or 'Together Everyone Achieves More' and discuss. Play 'Test Your Teamwork'. You need four or six benches and various sets of cards, spelling the word 'turnip'. In teams of six, each team should stand on a bench. Give each team member a letter from 'turnip'. On a signal, the children need to work together to get into the correct order to spell 'turnip'. If a team member falls off or swaps their card, their team is out. The first team to spell 'turnip' wins. Discuss what makes a good team member.

Practical Activities

- Using letters from the word 'team' ask the children to write some rules for working as a team, for example, 'T = take turns', 'E = each person is equal', 'A = ask for everyone's opinion', 'M = make sure you always listen to others'. These rules could be displayed around the classroom or school.

● Play 'Hoot the Hooter'. Place 16 hoops on the floor in four rows of four. Plot a route for the children to follow, but keep it secret. The children must try and find the correct route. One child at a time stands in a hoop; if they have chosen correctly, shake a football rattle and the child moves onto the next hoop. If it is the wrong hoop, hoot a hooter and the child goes to the back of the line and the next child tries. This can be made more complicated by adding rules, such as, 'no talking'.

● Play 'Thumbs Up, Thumbs Down'. Make a set of scenario cards, depicting either cooperative behaviour or uncooperative behaviour. Give each child a label with thumbs up on one side and thumbs down on the other. Invite two children to mime a scenario. Ask the others in the group to decide whether it deserves 'thumbs up' for cooperative behaviour or 'thumbs down' for uncooperative behaviour. Discuss their responses.

Art and Display

● Use paint and collage materials to create giant characters from the story and a huge turnip for display. Add labels about cooperation, such as, 'Why is teamwork important?'

● Practise observational drawings of fruit and vegetables and discover ways of adding detail and texture. Then challenge the children to paint a picture based on their drawings and mount them to create a class collage.

● Provide glue in a squeezy bottle with a fine nozzle, and silk material. Challenge the children to draw a piece of fruit or vegetable with the glue and colour with silk paints. Sew the work together to create a class wall hanging.

● Use paper in various shades to collage a piece of fruit or vegetable. These could be mounted separately or used to create a 'Funny Fruit Face'.

What would have happened if the characters in the story had not cooperated?

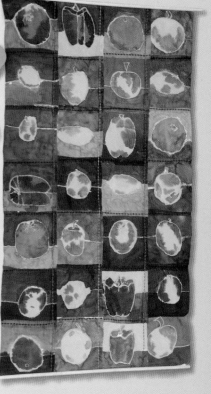

Cross-curricular Links

● **NUMERACY** – Investigate 'My turnip is as heavy as a …..'. Ask the children to find objects that are heavier, lighter or equal to the weight of a real turnip.

● **PE** – Arrange a sports day with the children organised in teams. Encourage them to work together.

● **LITERACY** – Challenge the children to write their own version of *The Enormous Turnip*, using a different setting and characters, for example, for 'The Highest Banana' the setting could be a jungle and the characters could climb on each others' shoulders.

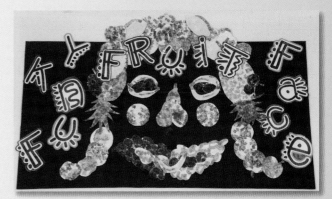

Face Your Feelings

Whole-class Starter

Learning Objective

- To recognise, name and deal with feelings in a positive way

- Use an owl puppet to introduce different feelings to the class. Explain that the owl is your friend but he keeps acting strangely and he is not sure what to do. The owl describes to the children a variety of situations and asks if they can help him recognise how he is feeling. For example, 'I keep crying when my mum is asleep and I keep hearing strange noises' or 'My brother took my share of the food that daddy brought us and I started to flap my wings and stamp my feet'. The children should help the owl to recognise and name his feelings.

- Brainstorm different types of feelings and create a mindmap to show these feelings. Ask the children how people behave when they are experiencing different feelings, they might suggest, 'When they are happy they smile' or 'When they are nervous they tremble'. Add these ideas as further branches on the mindmap.

- Play 'Face your Feelings' with a giant spinner showing different emotions. Give each pair of children a whiteboard and a pen. Spin the spinner and allow them one minute to discuss what might cause them to experience that feeling, for example, 'I feel worried when I can't find my mum', then record on the whiteboard.

- Play 'Freeze Frame that Feeling' with a set of 'feeling cards' such as 'happy', 'sad', 'angry' and 'lonely' in a bag. In a large space, with children in groups of three or four, each group must pull a feeling card out of the bag and create an appropriate 'freeze frame' for the rest of the class to identify.

Practical Activities

- With a small group of children talk about how we could express our feelings through calligrams. Explain that this is a shape poem. Show the children some examples of calligrams and ask them to design their own, illustrating different feelings.

- In pairs, ask the children to write an acrostic poem about a particular feeling. Here is an example:

  Left all alone
  One person with
  Nobody to love them
  Excluded not included
  Lost and all alone
  You don't know how it feels!

- In a drama session act out a 'Tunnel of Feelings'. As a group, read a suitable scenario or watch an appropriate video clip, then discuss. Invite one child to be the main character and talk about how they might be feeling. Other members of the group then form two lines to make a tunnel. The main character makes their way slowly through the tunnel, while the other children take turns to call out what they think the character is thinking and feeling.

Art and Display

- Chalk pastel a variety of faces showing different feelings for a class display. Add appropriate labels, such as 'What makes you feel happy?' and the children's responses, for example, 'I feel happy when I am with my family'.

- Create a collage of 'feeling' words using a variety of textures and colour tones.

- Study the artist Arcimboldo and look at the way he makes faces using different artefacts. Ask the children to design their own 'feelings face', for example, make a HAPPY face using anything that makes them happy, such as sunshine, ballet shoes, or football.

Cross-curricular Links

- **ICT** – Using a word processing package choose a 'feeling' word, such as 'sad' and find an appropriate size and font. Challenge the children to create a SAD picture using just that word: they could copy, paste, rotate and flip the word into a tear shape to achieve the desired effect.

- **RE** – Read or retell the Christian story of *Jonah and the Whale* from *The Bible Storybook* by Georgie Adams (Orion). Discuss how Jonah's feelings change and develop.

- **MUSIC** – Give the children percussion instruments to create sound effects for different feelings.

Go for Gold!

Whole-class Starter

- Jemima (you in role) enters the classroom, upset at not winning a medal at sports day. Explain that you are no good at running, nor can you jump or skip. During sports day you drew a picture which you thought was good but they never have a drawing competition on school sports day. Show the children the picture and ask them what they think. Ask the children if they are good at sports, and if not what are they good at.

- With the children sitting in a circle, give everyone a laminated gold medal and a whiteboard pen. Ask the children to write or draw a picture of something they are good at and then share their success with the group.

- In role as Jemima, explain that at school you are only good at drawing, but at home you are good at watering the garden, stroking grandma's cat, and making up games with friends. Ask the children to think about things they are good at when at school, home, with family, friends or on their own. Give them five sticky notes on which to draw a picture for each activity. Place large sheets of paper around the room titled 'school', 'home', 'family', 'friends' and 'self'. The children stick their notes on the appropriate sheet. Discuss their responses.

- Put the phrase 'No-one can do everything but everyone can do something' on the board. Discuss what this means. Ask the children to talk with a partner about things they are good at and why and how they know they are good at it. Encourage them to share their thoughts and feelings with each other. Ask each child to feed back to the class what their partner has said.

Learning Objective

- To think about ourselves and recognise what we are good at and to set ourselves simple goals

Practical Activities

- Give each child a copy of a trophy or shield divided into four sections. In each section they should draw a picture of something they are good at under different headings, such as 'home', 'school', 'family', 'friends' or 'self'.

- Play 'Search for Success'. Make a set of laminated letters for each child in the group, spelling 'success'. Make a set of jigsaw pieces that connect to make a phrase that encourages success, for example, 'Practice makes perfect' or 'If at first you don't succeed try, try again'. Place them face down for children to take turns in picking two pieces. If they make a quote, the child takes the first letter of 'success'; the first to complete the word wins.

- Play 'Go for Gold!' Place all the children's names in a bag. Invite each child to pick out a name. They must reflect on what the named child is good at and make that child a gold medal depicting their talent. At the end of the day invite the Headteacher into the class to present the medals to all the children.

- Give each child a medal-shaped booklet that opens out into sections. On the middle section ask the children to draw a self-portrait. Ask them to consider what they are good at and how it might help them in the future. On each of the other sections challenge the children to draw a picture of what they could achieve in the future, for example, 'I am a very good singer and might become a pop star' or 'I am good at maths and one day I might become a teacher'.

Art and Display

- Make giant gold medals for display using a paper plate, string, glue and gold spray.

- Make a clay trophy and spray gold.

- Invite the children to choose a phrase from the 'Search for Success' game (above) to illustrate and colour using a variety of media. Add these to the gold medal display.

Cross-curricular Links

- **LITERACY** – Challenge the children to write an acrostic poem based on 'success'. Here is an example:

    Shine like a star
    Understand your talents
    Can't does not exist
    Continue to try
    Everyone has a talent
    Share it with a friend
    Show the world your skills

- **NUMERACY** – Data handling: ask the children to survey the class and discover the range of talents. Record the information on a bar graph or chart.

- **CREATIVE ARTS** – Ask the children to prepare an entry for a class talent show.

Growing up

Whole-class Starter

- Take the role of an elderly person who has come to share her memories with the class, carrying in your bag a selection of items that relate to different stages of growing up, such as, a dummy, a toddler's toy, a young child's reading book, a lipstick, a gold locket. In chronological order show each item and 'recall' a story from 'your memories', for example, "I don't remember when I was a baby but my mother told me I used to throw my dummy out of the pram and then cry because I wanted it back again and again". You become tired and decide to pack away your things and return home. While tidying away, drop your bag, so everything falls out. Look sad and ask the children if they can help put your 'memories' back into the bag in the correct order.

- Play 'Triple It'. Make three sets of cards: one set with vocabulary relating to stages of life, for example, 'baby', 'toddler', 'child', 'teenager'; another set with corresponding pictures and a third set depicting objects associated with a particular age group, such as, a baby's rattle, a lipstick and a walking stick. Sit the children in a circle, with the cards face down in the middle. They take turns to select three cards; if they make a set they place them on the board. Continue until all the sets are complete.

- Listen to the song *Circle of Life* written by Elton John and Tim Rice. Ask the children what they think the phrase 'circle of life' means? Give each pair of children a circle of laminated card and a whiteboard pen. Ask them to talk about and draw what they understand the circle of life to be. Discuss with the whole class their thoughts and ideas.

Practical Activities

- Challenge the children to write a 'growing up' poem using rhyming couplets. Each couplet should be about a different stage of life and should rhyme, for example:

When I was a baby I used to wear a nappy,

When mum sang me a lullaby it made me really happy,

When I was a toddler I soon began to talk,

I learnt to crawl, then to waddle and finally to walk.

- Play 'It's Great to Grow up' in teams. Make a set of picture cards relating to the stages of growing up. Place the pictures on the board. Make a set of question cards, for example, 'Who is younger than a grandparent and older than a teenager?'. Collect items relating to the different stages, such as a toy, a set of car keys and a walking stick. A child from each team stands with their back to the board, while you read out a question. The first child to turn around and point to the correct picture collects an item from the first stage of growing up. Continue until one team has 'grown old'.

- Play 'Circle of Life'. Make a set of jigsaw pieces for each child in the group that connect to make a Circle of Life. On each section place a picture to represent a life stage. Make a set of statement cards relating to the different stages, some true, for example, 'a baby drinks milk', and some false: 'a child can drive a car'. Place the jigsaw pieces at the centre of the table and the statement cards in a bag. Children take turns to pick out a card; if the statement is correct they collect a piece of their jigsaw puzzle; if false, they miss a turn.

Art and Display

- Draw, paint and use collage materials to create large pictures representing life stages.

- Challenge children to sketch pen and ink portraits of how they think they would look when they are older.

- Collect together (or ask children to bring from home) small items to represent different life stages to create a circle of life mobile. They could hang, for example, a baby's rattle, a small toy, a CD and a set of keys from dowel rods and string.

Cross-curricular Links

- **HISTORY** – Make a timeline of life stages, using the vocabulary of time, including 'past', 'present' and 'future'.

- **LITERACY** – Children choose a life stage, such as 'toddler' as a subject for an acrostic poem. Pick some to add to the class display.

- **SCIENCE** – Investigate how in some ways we stay the same and in others we change as we grow up. Ask the children to measure a sample of five-year-olds and collect the data to consider the statement, 'Once you are five years old you grow to a metre tall'.

- **ICT** – Using a paint package, challenge the children to draw a life cycle diagram, including the different stages of growing up, captions and arrows.

Recipe for Friendship

Whole-class Starter

- Take the role of a mad chef who has discovered a secret recipe that will ensure everybody can make friends. The chef has a large saucepan and a big wooden spoon. Out of a bag, take an instruction that is needed in order to make a friend, for example, 'Sprinkle in a spoonful of sharing'; 'Mix in a bag full of laughter'; 'Stir in a cupful of generosity'. The phrases should be written on large cards to pin on a display board as you mix the recipe. Read the instructions aloud, then perform an appropriate action.

- After 'making' the concoction above, explain that all these ingredients are vital for making good friends. Ask the children (in pairs) to close their eyes while you remove one instruction from the board. Ask the children to open their eyes and discuss with their partner which ingredient is missing and why it cannot be left out. Repeat for all the ingredients.

- Play 'Bake a Cake', with the class in four teams. For each team you need a chef's hat and apron and a large laminated cake, divided into eight pieces. Make two sets of laminated cards, one bearing words or phrases that are qualities of a good friend, the other words or phrases that are not good friendship qualities, for example, 'will not share', 'pinches', 'takes your things'. Place the cards in a big saucepan in the middle of a large space. On a signal, the first member from each team puts on the chef's hat and apron, runs to the saucepan and collects a card. If it is a good friendship quality the team member collects a piece of cake and places it on the ground in front of their team. If it is a bad quality they do not collect a piece of cake. The next player then dons the hat and apron. The first team to complete their cake wins.

Practical Activities

- Challenge the children to write their own recipe for friendship.

- In small groups, play 'My Best Friend', based on the idea 'I went to the shop and bought….'. With the children in a circle, begin by saying, "I went to school and made a best friend who plays with me". The first child repeats and adds another thing that the friend would do, for example, '…plays with me and helps me fasten my coat'. Continue until someone makes a mistake; that child is out and the game begins again.

- Play 'Make Friends or Break Friends', with two sets of different coloured cards. On one set write words or phrases that either help you make friends or break friends, such as, 'shares toys', 'pulls hair'. On the other set write either 'make friends' or 'break friends'. Place both sets face down on the table. The children take turns to choose one card of each colour. If they match they keep them, if not, they replace them on the table. The winner collects the most pairs.

- In small groups, discuss the different types of friendships the children may have. Emphasise the fact that some people make lots of friends, some prefer to have one special friend, some have friends from both sexes, while for others their brother or sister is their best friend. Give each child a Friendship zig-zag book in the shape of a person. Ask them to write sentences about their friend and what makes them a good friend.

Art and Display

- Use collage materials and paint to create a large chef for display.

- In friendship pairs, ask the children to collage each other's faces using paper plates and a variety of materials, or make chalk pastel portraits.

- Ask the children to draw and colour a large picture of their friend and to label the parts of their body that make them a good friend, for example, 'My friend has a big heart to help her love me' or 'My friend has gentle hands that I can hold on to when I am scared'.

- Challenge the children to illustrate the ingredients from the chef's friendship recipe; a cupful of love could be illustrated as a large cup with hearts coming out of it.

Cross-curricular Links

- **FOOD TECHNOLOGY** – Ask the children to work in pairs or small groups to make a friendship cake.

- **LITERACY** – Write an acrostic poem for 'Friendship'.

- **DANCE** – In pairs, create a dance based on the Boyzone song, *You Needed Me*. As a follow-up, create a dance based on balances and support work to The Beatles song *With a Little Help from my Friends*.

The Tunnel

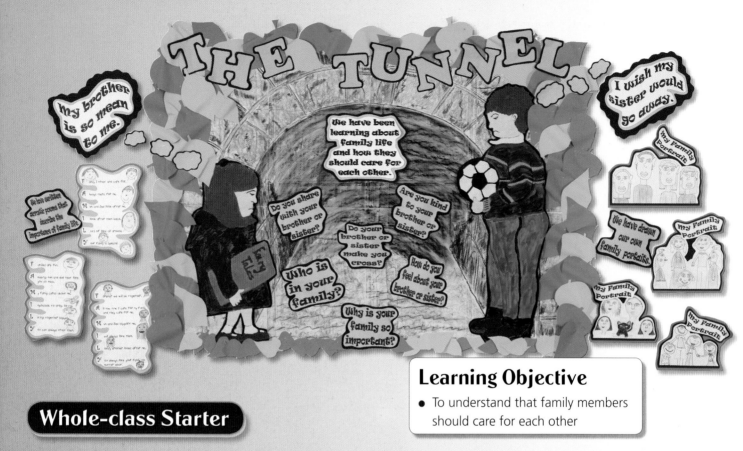

Learning Objective
- To understand that family members should care for each other

Whole-class Starter

- Read and discuss *The Tunnel* by Anthony Browne (Walker Books). Ask the children the following questions: "What is the theme of this story?"; "Who has brothers and sisters?"; "Do they get along?"; "Do they ever argue?"; "What do they argue about?"

- Make a set of giant picture cards based on illustrations from the story. Give each pair of children a whiteboard and a pen. Show them a selection of the pictures and ask them to discuss and write words to describe the characters, speech or thought bubbles describing what the characters are saying or thinking, and the changes in the relationship between the siblings.

- Play 'Fantastic Families'. Make a set of scenario cards, such as, 'Your brother has chicken pox and has to stay in bed' or 'Our sister has fallen out with her best friend and is sad'. Include situations that involve a potential argument between siblings, for example, 'Your sister breaks one of your toys on purpose'. Sit the children in a circle and spin a bottle. The child indicated picks a card and nominates a child to respond to the scenario. When the child answers appropriately the whole group shouts, "We are a fantastic family".

Practical Activities

- Make a Funny Family Flap Book. Give each child an A5 spiral-bound book in which the pages have been cut in half across the middle. Ask them to draw a member of their family on each page and add a phrase that explains how that person cares for their family. When the pages are turned, the pictures and the phrases will be mixed up, for example, 'I look after my mum... when she falls off the swing at the park'. For further amusement include a family pet.

- Play 'Family Fortunes'. Label a spinner with one letter from the word 'family' on each section. Give each child in the group a laminated sheet with 'family' written vertically along the edge. Children take turns to spin the spinner, and must write a phrase on their sheet describing how to care for their family. If the spinner lands on a letter they already have they miss a go. The first child to complete their acrostic poem wins. For an added dimension include a 'star' section on the spinner that means all the children must race to complete their acrostic poem.

- Play 'Family Skittles'. Label a set of skittles with the letters in 'family' and include a 'danger' skittle. Use the scenario cards from the whole-class starter session. Give each child a whiteboard and a pen. The children take turns to pick a card and say how they would help their family member. Then they bowl a ball and knock down as many skittles as they can. They write on their board the letters knocked down but if the 'danger' skittle falls they must rub their board clean and start again. The first to spell out 'family' wins.

- Ask the children to draw a portrait of a family member and write words around it to describe them. As an extension they could write in one colour things that they love about their family member and, in a different colour, traits that drive them crazy!

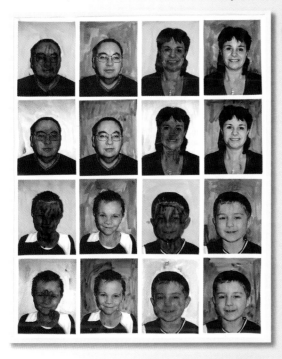

Art and Display

- Draw and use collage materials to create large pictures of the characters of Rose and Jack from the story for a display. Add labels to illustrate family relationships.

- Provide the children with card, wood, string and coloured pencils to create a family mobile.

- Using the artist Andy Warhol as a stimulus, ask the children to bring in pictures of family members' faces. Photocopy the pictures so they are black and white images, A5 size. Add colour to the pictures with primary colour inks. Assemble the pictures to make a family portrait in the style of Andy Warhol.

Cross-curricular Links

- **LITERACY** – Set up a small group as a Literature Circle to discuss the illustrations in *The Tunnel*. Alternatively, use letters from 'family' to think up phrases describing how family members care for each other and create a class acrostic.

- **DANCE** – Using the story as a stimulus, create a dance based on the siblings' journey. The children could work individually and in pairs, demonstrating different moods.

- **DRAMA** – Working in pairs, play 'Family Statues'. Pull a word out of a bag and ask the children to work together to create a statue to represent it, for example, 'ignoring', 'fighting', 'caring' or 'loving'.

Daisy

Learning Objective

● To understand what disability is and how people who have disabilities might feel, and some of the difficulties they face

Whole-class Starter

● Read *Susan Laughs* by Jeanne Willis (Red Fox). Discuss with the children what they understand when we say someone is 'disabled'. Ask the children to discuss with a partner the different kind of disabilities they think exist and any people they know with a disability. Work as a class to create a mindmap of their ideas.

● Ask the children to look closely at the pictures in *Susan Laughs* and think about how Susan feels. The pictures should offset any preconceived ideas the children may have that disabled children are unhappy because they are unable to do things. Discuss the fact that Susan is happy in all the pictures. Ask the children why they think this is so. Encourage the idea that Susan is happy because she is able to do all the things in the story even though she is disabled. Ask the children to discuss with a partner times when Susan might feel unhappy and frustrated about being disabled. Invite them to share their ideas and, as a class, make some suggestions about how her friends, family and community could help.

Practical Activities

● Ask the children to work in small groups to write an acrostic poem based on the word 'disability'. Use their ideas to create a large class acrostic that can be displayed in the classroom or school. (See Art and Display.)

● Challenge the children to think about ideas and guidance they could give to others about how to behave with a disabled friend, called Daisy. Emphasise that they should behave in the same way with Daisy as they would with an able-bodied person. These ideas can be made into a 'do's and don'ts' Daisy display.

Daisy deals with

Don't treat us Differently

It's not a disease.

Sometimes we need a little help

Actually we can do most things.

Because we use other parts of our body to help

Ican achieve anything I want to.

Learn to understand that we are not different

Impossible is not a word we understand!

The sky's the limit and

You can help us get there

What is disability?

How can we help people who have a disability?

What is learning disability?

What is physical disability?

What is sensory disability?

- Play 'Disabled Detectives.' Give each child a disabled detective badge, a magnifying glass, a laminated map of the school and a whiteboard pen. In small groups, the children walk around the school and identify on their map areas that cater for disabled people and those that do not. On their return to the classroom the children make suggestions of ways to improve their school environment to cater for the disabled community.

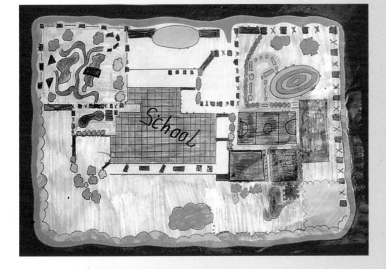

Art and Display

- Create a decorative display using paints and collage materials, based on the acrostic poem on 'Disability' (see Practical Activities). Add labels about different kinds of disability.

- Produce a leaflet on how to help a disabled friend. Ask the children to focus on one disability and illustrate captions explaining what they can do to help.

Cross-curricular Links

- **GEOGRAPHY** – Draw a map of the school and illustrate areas that cater for people with disability. This map could be used by the school to share with disabled visitors.

- **HISTORY** – Read and discuss the story of Braille. Invite a blind person into school to talk about how Braille affects their everyday life.

- **LITERACY** – Investigate forms of non-verbal communication, such as sign language, Morse code and semaphore (shown left). Challenge the children to invent their own form of non-verbal communication.

Elmer

Learning Objective

● To understand the ways in which people and cultures can vary and to learn to respect and celebrate these differences

Whole-class Starter

● Read and enjoy *Elmer* by David McKee (Red Fox). Discuss what made Elmer unhappy at the beginning of the story. What did he do to become the same as the other elephants? Did it make him happy to be the same? What happened at the end of the story? Ask the children to think in what ways Elmer is the same as, and how he differs from, the other elephants and mindmap their ideas. How does Elmer feel about being different? Is it a good or a bad thing?

● Ask the children to discuss in pairs ways in which they are similar to and different from others. Make two post boxes, one grey, one multi-coloured. Give each pair two pieces of elephant-shaped paper and ask them to write on one a way in which people are the same and on the other a way in which people differ and post them in the correct boxes. Empty the boxes and discuss their responses.

● Sitting in a circle, ask the children to think about how they are different and how that makes them special just like Elmer. If possible, give the first child a patchwork Elmer toy and ask them to pass him around the circle. Tell the children that while holding Elmer you would like them to share with the group how they are different and special.

● Talk about when Elmer felt different and felt excluded from the group. Discuss how sometimes when we are different, people make us feel bad about ourselves. They are often unkind and can make fun of us. Consider ways of dealing with feeling different or meeting somebody who is different from ourselves. As a class create a 'do's and don'ts' list, including phrases such as: 'Do ignore what people say'; 'Don't try and change for others'; 'Do be happy with yourself'; 'Don't listen to unkind words'.

Practical Activities

● Ask the children to write a letter to Elmer telling him why he should value being different and what makes him unique and special.

● Give each child a patchwork Elmer template. Ask them to write in each square how Elmer was different. This activity could be repeated by asking the children to write how people can be different. Encourage them to think about skin colour, religion, size, disabilities and age.

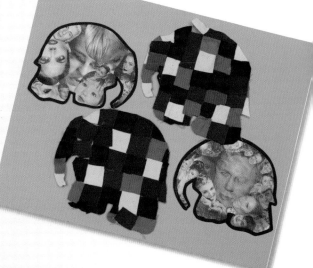

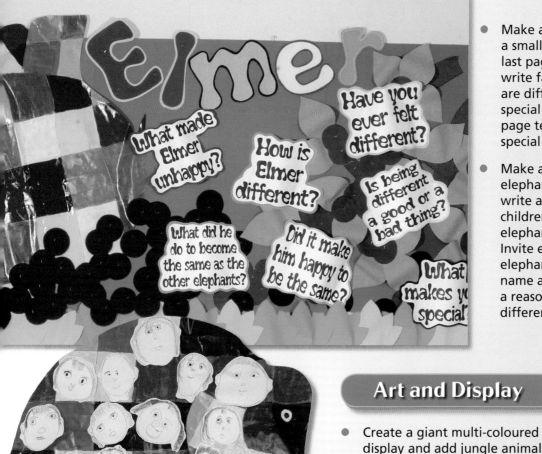

- Make a zig-zag book with a small mirror taped to the last page. Ask the children to write facts about why they are different, beginning 'I am special because…'. On the final page tell them to write 'I am special because I am ME!'.

- Make a set of small laminated elephants. On each elephant write a child's name. Sit the children in a circle and place the elephants in a box in the middle. Invite each child to pick out an elephant. The child reads the name and shares with the group a reason why that person is different and therefore special.

Art and Display

- Create a giant multi-coloured collage Elmer for display and add jungle animals. Add labels to celebrate difference.

- Cut out an elephant shape from hessian and challenge the children to sew colourful patchwork squares on to it.

- Make a colour wheel using different shades of the same colour. Discuss with the children how all the colours on the wheel are essentially the same but different.

- Ask the children to draw a self-portrait. Arrange the portraits on a giant elephant-shaped piece of paper in patchwork squares to look like Elmer. Alternatively they could cut out people's faces from magazines to stick on an elephant or person-shaped piece of paper.

Cross-curricular Links

- **ICT** – Ask the children to design an 'Elmer Day' elephant, using a paint program. Use a multi-media program to publish the animated story of Elmer.

- **GEOGRAPHY** – Discuss with the children the variety of different ethnic groups that exist in the world, the country, and their school.

- **RE** – Find religious stories that relate to the issues in *Elmer*, for example, Christian tales such as *The Prodigal Son* or *The Good Samaritan* from *My Own Book of Bible Stories* by Pat Alexander (Lion).

David and Goliath

Learning Objective

- To understand that bullying is wrong and how to get help to deal with bullying

Whole-class Starter

- Brainstorm with the children ways to behave that are nice and not nice. In role as a classmate, tell the class you are upset because some children have been unkind to you. Say that you are being bullied and do not know what to do. Ask your classmates for help. Give each child a sticky note and ask them to write one thing that you could do that would help you. Discuss the children's responses.

- Read the story of *David and Goliath* (from *The Bible Storybook* by Georgie Adams (Orion). Talk with the children about how they would feel if they were David, how they would behave, what they think of Goliath and why David was scared of him. Emphasise that what Goliath did was not a nice way to behave and how these actions make other people feel. In pairs, let the children discuss a time when they have been scared of someone and why, and what happened as a consequence.

- Invite Goliath (you in role) into the classroom, so the children can 'hot seat' (interview) him. Then, in role as David, tell the children you are upset about your own actions at the end of the story. Talk to the children about alternative courses of action.

- Learn the 'Bully song' to the tune of *Frère Jacques*, repeating each line:

There's a bully	First ignore them	We are happy
In our school	Then tell Miss	School is safe
Always being nasty	She'll sort out the problem	No more bully
What shall we do?	Bully has gone	(School name) is great!

- Play 'Knock Down Bully'. Build a tower from a large Jenga set. Challenge children to think of ways of dealing with bullies. For each idea remove a block.

Practical Activities

- Play 'Freeze Frame Role-Play' in small groups. Invite the children to re-enact the story of *David and Goliath*. 'Freeze frame' the role-play at different intervals and ask the children to say what the character is thinking or feeling.

- Draw a poster illustrating how we like to be treated, or design an anti-bullying poster.

- Write an anti-bullying acrostic poem and perform it to the class.

- Play 'What should you do?' with children in groups of two or three. Make a set of scenario cards, for example, 'Someone steals your bag of crisps and says they will hurt you if you tell'. Give each group a card and ask them to re-enact the scenario to the class. The children then discuss the situation and what the child should do to resolve the problem.

Art and Display

- Use collage materials and paint to create a large David and Goliath display. Add appropriate labels about bullying.

- Design a 'Fight the bully' shield. Split the shield into four sections and draw symbols illustrating nice ways to behave. Use chalk pastels to add colour.

- Use paint and collage materials to design an anti-bullying symbol for the school.

Cross-curricular Links

- **RE** – Read the Christian story of *Joseph and his Multi-coloured Coat* from *My Own Book of Bible Stories* by Pat Alexander (Lion). Discuss what makes bullies bully.

- **MUSIC** – Challenge children in small groups to compose an anti-bullying song or rap.

- **LITERACY** – Ask the children to write their own bullying story.

The Paperbag Prince

Learning Objective

- To understand how rubbish can harm the local and natural environment and how by recycling we can take some responsibility for our environment

Whole-class Starter

- Using *The Paperbag Prince* by Colin Thompson (Red Fox) as a basis, retell the story in your own words. Discuss the effect the rubbish dump had on the town and on the animals and plants that lived there. Ask the children why the man was nicknamed 'The Paperbag Prince'. What did he do to help the environment? Ask if the children do anything to help their environment like the Paperbag Prince. Discuss their responses.

- Introduce the terms 'reduce', 'reuse' and 'recycle' by showing the children big visual signs and giving examples of each. Label a spinner with these three words. Give each child a whiteboard and a pen. Spin the spinner and ask the children to write or draw something they do at home that corresponds to the word chosen. If the spinner lands on 'reuse', they might write, 'At home we reuse carrier bags as bin liners'.

- Play 'Race to Reduce, Recycle, Reuse'. Place the big signs (see above) around the classroom. Give each child an object or a card with a picture. On a given signal, the children must run and stand by an appropriate sign for their object. Ask the children to explain their choices, for example, for a banana skin they could run to 'recycle' as it can be recycled as compost.

Practical Activities

- Play 'Rescue the Rubbish.' Make a class 'rubbish dump' using a variety of objects that may be reused, recycled or reduced, plus some real rubbish. Put four hoops around the pile, labelled 'reuse', 'recycle', 'reduce' and 'real rubbish'. Give the children one minute to walk around the pile and reflect on which objects belong in which hoop. Then cover the rubbish pile and the children must take it in turns to recall one piece of rubbish and identify where it should go. If a child repeats an object or cannot think of a new one, they are out. The last child left in wins.

Recycling Rap

RECYCLE
YO! YO! YO!
Don't chuck that rubbish
GO! GO! GO!
Keep the world as clean as you can
REMEMBER
Recycle as much as you can!
Keep that land as clean as you can
REMEMBER
Reuse as much as you can!
Try and improve the air that you use
Plant trees so that you can breathe
YO! Do it now so the world won't end.
Do it every weekend!
RECYCLE! REUSE! REDUCE!

- Teach the children a 'Reuse, Reduce and Recycle' rap (see left and page 72), then challenge them to compose their own version.

- Play 'Recognise the Rubbish'. Give each child a colour photocopied picture of a rubbish dump and ten small laminated discs marked 'R'. The children take turns to roll a 1-6 dice, then cover on their picture the corresponding number of objects at the dump that could be recycled, reused or reduced rather than dumped. The first person to get rid of all their discs wins.

- Make an environmentally friendly leaflet or poster highlighting ways in which people can improve their environment by reusing, recycling and reducing waste rather than dumping it. Encourage the children to combine word play and illustrations, for example, for 'Recycle' the prefix 'Re' could be followed by a picture of a bicycle made up out of recyclable materials, such as toilet rolls, bottles, teabags, newspapers.

Art and Display

- Paint and use collage materials to create a giant 'Paperbag Prince' display. Add appropriate labels from the story.

- Using Colin Thompson's illustrations as a stimulus, challenge the children to draw their own rubbish dump following his style.

- Provide a selection of recyclable material for the children to create a sculpture of their choice.

Cross-curricular Links

- **DRAMA** – Play 'It's not a Paper Bag'. Put an ordinary paper bag in the middle of a circle of children. Invite them to take turns to pick up the bag and say 'It's not a paper bag, it's a....', using their imagination to reinvent the bag as something else, for example, a hat, glove, fairy's wing.

- **MUSIC** – Challenge the children to create their own musical instruments from various recyclable materials and form a percussion band.

- **DESIGN & TECHNOLOGY** – Design and make a caravan for the Paperbag Prince, including fittings and fixtures that have been recycled or reused from the rubbish dump.

The Litter Queen

Whole-class Starter

Learning Objective

- To understand how litter can harm the local environment and ways to help solve the litter problem

- In role dressed as the title character from *The Litter Queen* by Roderick Hunt (OUP), empty bins and scatter rubbish all around the classroom. Explain to the children that they are now your 'litter servants' and their job is to spread rubbish and spoil all the pretty places in the world. Tell them you are fed up with all these people that recycle and keep the country clean; you see recycling bins and people collecting litter everywhere you go and it makes you cross. Say you are going to give each of them a bag of litter to spread around their school. Ask the children what they think; they should protest and tell you that it would be wrong. Encourage them to explain their reasoning, feigning horror at their responses so they have to clarify what they mean.

- As Litter Queen, give each pair of children a sticky note and ask them to write one reason why dropping litter is bad for the environment. Read out their responses and ask why no-one has informed you of this before.

- Play 'Rubbish Removal'. Spell the word 'litter' down the side of the board and together write an acrostic poem to help people understand how bad litter is. In pairs, using a whiteboard, children think of a phrase relating to each letter of the word 'litter'. Look at their ideas and choose one for each letter. Each time they complete a line of the poem they all must go and collect a piece of litter (previously dropped by the Litter Queen) to put in the rubbish bin. By the end of the poem the classroom should be litter-free.

Practical Activities

- Ask the children to make posters to put around the school and local community to reduce the litter problem. Alternatively, they could design a leaflet explaining why littering is not acceptable and ways to remove rubbish from their local environment.

- Discuss what is meant by a 'litterbug' and ask the children (in pairs) to create their own giant litterbug out of rubbish.

- Play 'Lose that Litter' with a set of scenario cards, for example, 'You find an empty tin can on a park bench and put it in the bin, collect three pieces of litter' or 'You drop a piece of litter out of the car window, miss a go'. Give each group a pile of rubbish in a large space and a 'rubbish grabber'. The children take turns to pick a scenario card out of a rubbish bin and follow the instructions. The first team to clear their rubbish pile wins.

- Create a school Garbage Gang to be responsible for keeping the premises litter-free. Design and make a badge for the gang to wear.

Art and Display

- Paint and use collage materials to create a giant Litter Queen for display.

- Using Arcimboldo as a stimulus, ask the children to create their own picture of the Litter Queen from litter.

- Make observational drawings of litter.

- Draw and paint giant litterbugs.

Cross-curricular Links

- **LITERACY** – Read *The Litter Queen* by Roderick Hunt but stop at the point where Chip is fed up about spreading litter. Ask the children to finish the story.

- **MUSIC** – Challenge children (in groups) to make their own musical litter acrostic with actions.

- **ASSEMBLY** – Introduce a litter-themed assembly, based on any appropriate story. Introduce the Garbage Gang and present them with their badges. Have a litter collecting day and distribute stickers to children in return for collecting litter.

Crab's Kingdom

Learning Objective

- To understand that there are different types of pollution and how they affect our environment.

Whole-class Starter

- Talk to the class about a recent wildlife walk you took. Tell them you went to feed the ducks at your local pond and were horrified to find it was full of rubbish and the ducks all gone. Then you visited the beach and were saddened to discover a dead seagull that had been killed by an oil spillage. You decided to go for a picnic instead at a favourite beauty spot, only to find a new road had been built close by! The traffic noise had driven all the wildlife away and exhaust fumes from cars meant that no-one could picnic there any more. Explain that you are sick and tired of all this pollution. Ask the class if they know what pollution means and explain that there are three types – air, water and noise.

- Make a set of cards with pictures and words of different examples of air, water and noise pollution, such as, aeroplane, radio and oil can. Place three hoops, labelled 'air', 'water' and 'noise' in the centre of a circle of children. Give each child a card and ask them to put it in the appropriate circle. Discuss their decisions.

- Label three large sheets of paper 'air pollution', 'water pollution' and 'noise pollution' and spread them around the room. Give each child a sticky note and a card from the previous activity. Ask them to read their card, decide what type of pollution is depicted and write on the note what effect it would have on the environment. They then place the card and note on the appropriate sheet of paper.

- Read the story *Crab's Kingdom* from *Together Today: Themes and Stories for Assembly* by Robert Fisher (Collins Educational). Discuss the ending and what the little boy did to solve the crab's problem. Play 'What's the Solution to the Pollution?' with the children in threes. Give each group a whiteboard, a pen and a pollution card (see above). Ask each group to write a solution to their pollution card.

Practical Activities

- Challenge the children to write a newspaper report about one of the local pollution issues you encountered on your wildlife walk.

- Play 'Pollution Pelmanism' with two sets of cards, one depicting pollution issues, the other with corresponding solutions. The children take turns to pick two cards. If they match, the children keep the cards. To make it more exciting add in some 'danger' cards; if a child picks one they either miss a turn or put all their cards back.

- Play 'Protect us from Pollution'. The children should make their own A3 pollution scene board and include all aspects of pollution – air, water and noise. Make a set of small cards labelled 'air', 'water' and 'noise' and put them in a bag. Give each child a whiteboard pen. The children take turns to pick out a card and cross off the corresponding pollution picture on their board. As an extension you could ask the children to either write or give you an explanation of how to prevent each form of pollution. The first child to cross out all the different types of pollution wins.

- Using *Crab's Kingdom* as a stimulus, challenge the children to create a cartoon strip to retell the story.

Art and Display

- In pairs, ask the children to draw and chalk pastel a large 'before and after' pollution picture.

- Make large countryside and seaside signs that give rules on how to keep the environment safe from pollution.

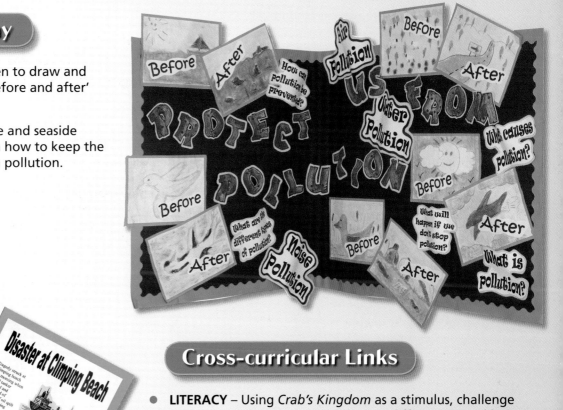

Cross-curricular Links

- **LITERACY** – Using *Crab's Kingdom* as a stimulus, challenge the children to write a new story about a different animal being affected by pollution.

- **GEOGRAPHY** – Draw a map of the school grounds and identify areas that could be affected by pollution.

- **ICT** – Using a desktop publishing package, children could learn to publish their work in a newspaper format.

Through my Window

Whole-class Starter

- Using *Window* by Jeannie Baker (Walker Books), play some gentle music and show the children each picture in the story. Give each child a whiteboard and a pen. Ask them to record the changes that occur in each picture. Discuss what they notice about the pictures and the changes to the environment.

- Talk about why environments change, different types of environments and who or what thrives there. Play 'Environments for Everyone'. Make two sets of cards, a blue set depicting different environments, such as a pond, woodland or a house, and a red set of different living things, for example, a person, frog, hedgehog or flower. Place the cards face down in the middle of a circle of (seated) children who take turns to pick up a red and blue card. If they match they keep the cards, if not they put them back.

- Discuss who created the changes in the environments in the book and the concept of man-made and natural environments. Ask the children if they can explain the difference. Play 'Natural or Man-made'. Make a set of cards depicting man-made and natural environments. Stand the children in two long lines in the middle of a large square; one line is the 'Natural' team, the other the 'Man-made' team. Show the children a picture of either a man-made or a natural environment, for example, a house or pond. That team must run as fast as they can to the edge of the square while the other team tries to catch them. If caught they are out; the object is to catch all the opposing team members.

Learning Objective

- To consider how changes to the environment affect our world and living things

Practical Activities

- Using the first and penultimate pictures from the story, ask the children to spot the differences and discuss the advantages and disadvantages of each change to the environment.

- Give each child a window-shaped zig-zag book. Challenge them to draw the view from their bedroom or classroom window. On the following pages they could draw changes that might happen in the future to change the view.

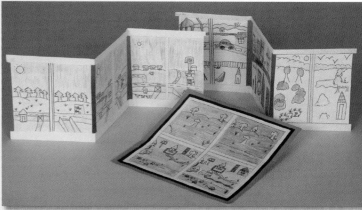

- In small groups, give each child a badge labelled 'Town Planner'. Tell them their job is to plan a New Town. As Town Planners they must consider the needs of the people who live in the town as well as the plants and animals in the environment. Give the group an A2 piece of paper on which to design a town layout. As an extension, ask the children to give reasons for their decisions.

- Provide a small group with the book *Window* by Jeannie Baker. Ask them to study the pictures carefully and identify the natural and man-made changes in each picture.

Art and Display

- Set children a homework task of photographing the view from their bedroom window. Challenge them to use the photograph to create their own collage in the style of Jeannie Baker.

- Talk about the use of shades of green in the book. Give each child a card with a strip of double sided sticky tape on. Take them for a walk around the school grounds to collect as many shades of green from the environment as they can, and to stick them on their cards. In the classroom ask the children to colour mix shades of green from their card.

- Provide a variety of collage materials for children to make a mobile of natural and man-made objects.

Some of these changes are good but some are bad.

Cross-curricular Links

- **SCIENCE** – Give each child a stick with an elastic band wrapped around it, called a 'Journey stick'. Take the children on a walk around the school grounds looking for natural things in the environment. They record their journey by collecting samples and attaching them to their stick.

- **LITERACY** – Using pictures from the story, ask the children to write speech bubbles or text for each picture. Encourage them to consider what the character in the story would be thinking about all the changes.

- **DESIGN & TECHNOLOGY** – Ask the children to design and make their own natural wildlife area from junk materials.

Potty about Pets

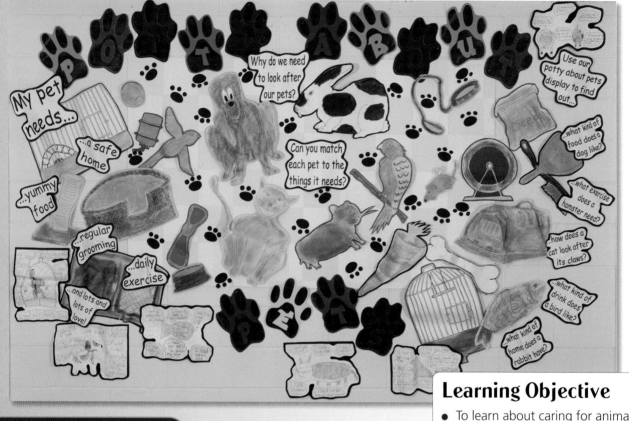

Learning Objective

- To learn about caring for animals and how to be responsible for pets

Whole-class Starter

- Read and enjoy *Arthur* by Amanda Graham and Donna Gynell (Era Books). Talk about why Arthur was sad. Show the last picture of Arthur with his new owner. Discuss the fact that Arthur has finally found someone to love and care for him. Ask the children what the little girl now needs to do to care for Arthur properly. Mindmap their ideas.

- Ask the children whether all animals' needs are the same. Display giant pictures around the room based on animals from the story and give each child three sticky notes. Challenge them to think about the needs of the different animals, for example, 'Dogs like a bone to chew' or 'Cats need a scratching post' and to write on each note a suggestion of how the little girl in the story should care for a particular animal. Invite the children to stick their responses onto the appropriate picture and discuss them as a class.

- Play 'Pet Pandemonium'. Make four sets of different coloured cards: one set with pet pictures; the second set, different pet's food; the third set showing the exercise different pets need; the fourth set depicting pets' homes. Give each child a card and let them walk around the room to find their 'team mates'. You could play *Who Let the Dogs Out?* by Baha Men as an accompaniment.

Practical Activities

- Play 'Pamper a Pet', with the cards from 'Pet Pandemonium' (above). Let each child choose a pet picture and place the rest of the cards in a bag. The children take turns to pick a card. If the card corresponds to their pet they put it on their animal card, if not, they put it back. The first to collect a set wins.

- Play 'Pet Predicament', using the pet picture cards from the 'Pet Pandemonium' game and a headband. Nominate a child to wear the headband. Attach a card to the headband (without the child seeing it). The wearer asks questions about their pet that can only be answered 'yes' or 'no'. Once s/he guesses the pet correctly the headband goes to another child.

- Ask the children to draw a picture of their own pet or a pet they would like. Around the edge of the picture they should write captions beginning with 'I need.....'. So a picture of a dog might be captioned 'I need to be taken for a walk every day'.

- Challenge the children to make a Pet Fact File. Encourage them to find out about lots of different types of pets and their needs, including stick insects, spiders and snakes.

Art and Display

- Draw, paint and use collage materials to create large pictures of pets and their needs for display.

- Ask the children to use a photograph to help them draw and paint a pet portrait using their observational skills.

- Fashion a pet handpuppet from a sock and other materials.

- Create a pet mask with a paper plate and collage materials.

Cross-curricular Links

- **DESIGN & TECHNOLOGY** – Design and build an imaginative ideal home for a pet.

- **ICT** – Challenge the children to create a slide show presentation on their chosen pet and present it to the class.

- **LITERACY** – Have a pet show (with parental permission). Invite children to bring their pet (or toy animal) to school and use their speaking and listening skills to present their pet and talk about how they look after it. Alternatively, create an alphabet of pets.

- **MATHS** – Carry out a survey on the different pets children have and record the information as a graph, tally or pie chart.

Oi! Get off our Train

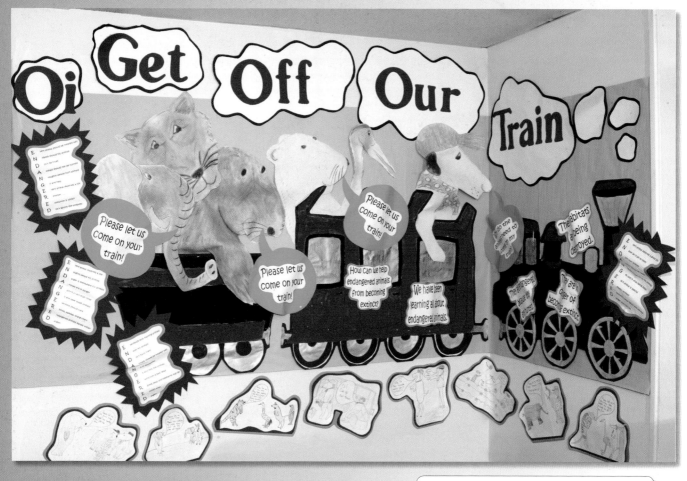

Whole-class Starter

- Read and enjoy *Oi! Get off our Train* by John Burningham (Red Fox). Discuss what the story is about. Why do the animals want to get on the train? How does the little boy help them? Explain to the children that the animals in the book are 'endangered' because they are in danger of becoming extinct. Discuss what 'extinct' means.

- Give each pair of children a whiteboard and a pen and show them a picture of one of the animals from the story. The children should write down why that animal is in danger of becoming extinct. Ask if they know of any other animals that are endangered, and why.

- Play 'Animal Extinction'. Make a set of cards depicting endangered animals, and another set with the corresponding reason why each animal is endangered, for example: 'elephant', and 'hunted for their ivory tusks'. Sit the children in a circle and spin a bottle. The child indicated comes out and selects two cards. If they match they shout "Animal Extinction" and keep the cards; if not, they put the cards back.

- Play 'O! Get off our Train', with the cards from 'Animal Extinction' (above). You need enough cards and chairs for each class member. Arrange the chairs as a train and stick the endangered animal cards under the seats. Place the 'reason' cards in a bag. As in musical chairs, children move in a line around the chairs while suitable music plays; when it stops the children sit quickly on a chair. Pick a card out of the bag and read out the 'reason'. The children look under their chairs to discover if they have the correct endangered animal. If so, they are 'extinct' (out). The last child remaining wins.

Learning Objective

- To understand that some animals are in danger of becoming extinct, what that means and how we can help

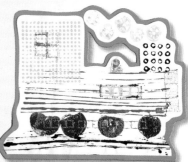

Practical Activities

- Challenge the children to write an acrostic poem about ENDANGERED animals.

- Play 'Animal Aid Train'. Make a set of A3 boards in the shape of a train, with at least six carriages (one set per child). Spread the endangered animal cards (from previous games) face up on the table. Put the 'reason' cards in a bag. Children take turns to pick out a 'reason' card, find the corresponding animal card and place it on their train. For variety, several 'hunter' cards could be added to the bag. If a child picks a 'hunter' card they lose all their animals and must start again. The first child to fill their train wins.

- Play 'Stop Extinction' in a large space. Choose five different endangered animals and make an animal card for each child to attach to their clothes. Ask them to stand in a circle and close their eyes. Tap one child (or more) on the head to be the 'hunter', so nobody knows who it is. The children open their eyes and move around the space. On the words "Hunt hunter hunt!" the hunter(s) must tag as many 'animals' as they can in ten seconds. The tagged animals must sit down. When the time is up the animals look around to see who has been tagged. If all of one species has been tagged they are 'extinct' and out. If some of them remain, then they can all stay in the game. Repeat until just one species remains and declare them the winners.

- Ask children to rewrite their own *Oi! Get off our Train* story. Give each child a train-shaped zig-zag book. On each carriage they should draw an endangered animal and their reason for wanting to board the train.

Art and Display

- Paint and use collage materials to create a giant train and a selection of endangered animals for display.

- Challenge the children to use chalk pastels to recreate a picture from the story in the style of John Burningham.

- Print a train picture, using a variety of materials, for example, cotton reels for wheels, rulers for tracks.

Cross-curricular Links

- **LITERACY** – Design a poster showing why animals should be protected.

- **ICT** – Make an animated version of the story, using moving pictures and sound effects.

- **GEOGRAPHY** – Using a world map, find areas around the world where animals are endangered. Ask the children to make drawings of animals for markers.

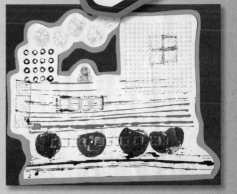

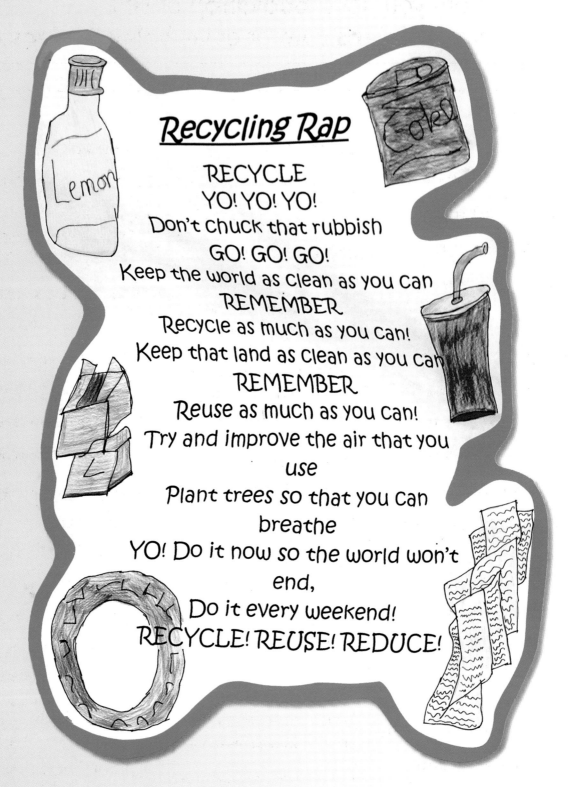

Recycling Rap

RECYCLE
YO! YO! YO!
Don't chuck that rubbish
GO! GO! GO!
Keep the world as clean as you can
REMEMBER
Recycle as much as you can!
Keep that land as clean as you can
REMEMBER
Reuse as much as you can!
Try and improve the air that you use
Plant trees so that you can breathe
YO! Do it now so the world won't end,
Do it every weekend!
RECYCLE! REUSE! REDUCE!

The Paperbag Prince (page 61)